Blackberry Rain

A collection of memories of adventures
from everyday life at the
Children's Home in
Winston-Salem, North Carolina
1947 to 1959

Oleg & Stella, all the very best, always!

Gilmer and Graham Murdock

ISBN 978-1-4507-4144-6

Editor: Kirsten McBride

Book and Cover Design: Vivian Strand

This book is designed in Clarendon and New Century Schoolbook.

Printed in the United States of America.

Dedication

This book is dedicated to the many caring people who had very little, yet found a way to reach deep and give us what they sorely needed themselves. They represented the strength of our nation. Of course, many others with greater means also contributed immensely either directly or indirectly to our well-being. And then there was the staff. There were no finer people on this earth – the campus staff, the farm staff, the teachers, the incredibly committed Home Mothers.

God has a special place for those who, by their kind deeds and sacrifice, permitted so many children to grow, learn, and accomplish.

Matthew 25:40
"And the King shall answer and say to them,
Truly I say to you,
Inasmuch as you have done it to one
of the least of these my brothers, you have done it to me."

Sam, Jerry, Gilmer, and Graham Murdock, just before going to the Children's Home.

Preface

In 1947, four young brothers, Gilmer, Graham, Jerry, and Sam Murdock, were placed in the care of the Children's Home in Winston-Salem, North Carolina – a privately funded Methodist home for children. Our older brothers had been away at war, and our mom had just died giving birth to her twelfth child, a son, who was adopted by an uncle in Iowa. Placing us in the Children's Home was not an easy decision for our father, or our older brothers and sister, as was the case for many parents who found it necessary to place their children into the care of the Home. In the twelve years during which we were residents at the Home, we did not lose contact with our family. They visited regularly, and we spent our summer vacations with them. We are blessed to have had the opportunity to be members of the Children's Home family.

Many people considered this an orphanage when, in spirit, it was quite the contrary. Children, whose parents struggled to make ends meet but who were loving and sensible and had strong Christian beliefs, were the proud residents of the Home – a place where adventures were the norm and dreams were made into reality.

Few, if any, of us who grew up at the Children's Home doubt that we were blessed. Not only did we receive a great education and developed many good and lasting friendships, we also received all the love, clothes, food, shelter, and care that anyone could hope for. We were taught the value of hard work, honesty, trust, and faith in Christ, and were instilled with a quiet determination to stand shoulder to shoulder with others in need. This "wealth" has lasted us a lifetime and has been passed on to following generations.

It might seem odd to an outsider that the Children's Home boys and girls firmly believed there were many people less fortunate than they were. But, regardless of social, political, or financial status, we recognized that everyone did not possess the "wealth" we possessed. The net of it all was the miracle of discovering the meaning of true happiness at an early age and holding onto this throughout our lives – knowledge that "ownership" does not constitute "happiness."

The Children's Home, a charge of the Methodist of the Western North Carolina Conference, was supported financially in greatest part through private donations, and in part by the work of the residents of the Home. All the buildings at the Home were named after philanthropic benefactors, gracious people who cared for children. Major contributions over the years also came from countless five-cent contributions, straight from the soul of people who themselves were desperately struggling to make ends meet for their families.

This is a measure of the strength of our country and embodies the spirit of what made us a great nation. The residents of the Children's Home are an excellent study in what could be accomplished for children through a well-managed, disciplined, and caring environment, peppered with hard work, hard play, and delivering a solid education to each child. Our mentors and teachers were very special people. They were our guides through each stage of our growth.

Preface

At any given time while we lived at the Home, there were between 400 and 450 other kids, evenly divided between boys and girls. Our living quarters, approximately twenty-three cottages, were situated on a magnificent campus of about forty acres, with two running creeks. The entire contiguous land area embraced 360 acres, with over 625 acres of land total holdings. Each cottage was made of the finest brick, with a slate roof and a coal-fired furnace. Many had porches from which we could enjoy the beautiful North Carolina scenery. In addition to cottages, which housed children based upon age, there was a central dining hall, an infirmary, a central laundry, a large gymnasium, two swimming pools, a recreation hall, and a private elementary school.

In addition to the campus laundry facility, we had a room for fitting and altering clothes, and a shoe store for exchanging, repair, and fitting of shoes. To sustain ourselves, we ran a truck farm where we grew all our own fruits and vegetables, including a large and productive cannery. Our dairy products came from 125 to 150 Holstein milk cows. We produced our own milk, including pasteurizing and homogenizing it. Older boys worked on the "big farm" where we raised all the crops necessary to grind and mix our own feed for our beef cattle, milk cows, and pigs. The mixing of feed was done in our mill. We also slaughtered and put up our own meat.

All the while we were doing the chores, we were getting a great education, building character, and for the most part staying out of trouble. These were wonderful times in the South, times of change and occasionally challenge. The following stories will give a glimpse of the mischief we used to get into and the fun we had. The book includes real events and is tempered with some pain of growing up without our real parents, but rejoices in growing up with hundreds of brothers and sisters, guided by wonderful people committed to our everyday well-being.

Blackberry Rain took us over six years to write. We spent most of that time laughing so hard we were in tears. There are so many fond memories of the wonderful staff and our hundreds of Children's Home brothers and sisters. We hope you enjoy our book, but most of all we hope this gives you a reason to support Children's Homes around the world.

> *The Lord bless you, and keep you;*
> *The Lord make His face shine on you,*
> *And be gracious to you;*
> *The Lord lift up His countenance upon you,*
> *And give you peace.*

The following events are written from two boys' perspectives, but they could be echoed by any one of the other boys and girls at the Children's Home. (Unless otherwise stated, Graham is the narrator.) Throughout, names have been changed, in most cases to protect the guilty.

Each story begins with a statement taken from *The Home Chronicles*, authored by O. V. (Pop) Woosley, superintendent. The word "superintendent" may sound a bit misleading here. Pop was a mentor and friend, and an example of the good in the souls of extraordinary people. Mom and Pop Woosley were the essence of the Children's Home, exceptional people leading an exceptional staff. They knew every child by name and worked hard to ensure that each child was well taken care of. Whenever they walked around the campus, they looked like Pied Pipers, followed by a string of kids. All the children trusted and loved them. That's why we all called them Mom and Pop. Through the decades, *The Home Chronicles* were a reflection of the purpose, activities, and philosophies of the Children's Home set against the backdrop of wars, the Depression, Prohibition, many presidents, the unification of churches, and the youth and old age of staff and children alike.

Preface

Gilmer and Graham Murdock.

O. V. (Pop) Woosley, Superintendent 1930 -1954.

Aerial view of the grounds of the Children's Home.

Names of Cottages by Age Group

Girls

William Neal Reynolds Building	Baby Cottage	Babies up to 5 years old
Smith	6 & 7 years old	2nd graders
Cornelius	8 & 9 years old	3rd & 4th graders
High Point	10 & 11 years old	5th graders
Julia Higgins	12 & 13 years old	6th & 7th graders
Lucy Stultz		
Stockton	13 & 14 years old	Some 7th graders
		8th & 9th graders
James A. Gray	15-18 years old	11th &12th graders

Boys

William Neal Reynolds Building	Baby Cottage	Babies up to 5 years old
Anna Hanes	6 & 7 years old	2nd graders
Norfleet	8 & 9 years old	3rd & 4th graders
Tise 1	10 & 11 years old	5th graders
Tise 2	12 & 13 years old	6th & 7th graders
Duke	14 & 15 years old	8th & 9th graders
John Neal*	16 & 17 years old	10th & 11th graders
Wren	17 & 18 years old	12th graders

Became John W. Hanes when torn down.

Table of Contents

The central dining hall.

INTRODUCTION:

Daily Life

"We here at the Children's Home have a minimum amount of supervision, both of workers and of children. We work on the assumption that a certain amount of freedom and individual expression are necessary in the cultivation of one's judicial temperament. We do not proceed in a lock step fashion. With such a system in operation it becomes necessary to have frequent conferences in order to understand the general trend of things.

Our Home Mothers meet regularly once a week at which time we discuss ways and means of directing our family. In these meetings our emphasis does not deal with problem children but with the problems of the children. A similar procedure is used with our department heads. It is our aim to keep a step ahead of our children, to anticipate their needs and to be in a position to direct them in the use of them. Such meetings are not built for complaints but for direction. In them there is lots of talk."

Blackberry Rain

All the children at the Home had a job to do, and everyone took pride in doing it to the best of their ability. In our case, we could get up at 3 a.m. and milk cows, or get up at 4 a.m. and help our friend Ward check traps.

The cow milking routine was required of just about all the boys at one time or other. It consisted of walking up to the dairy, chasing the cows from the lower lot to the milk barn and then into their assigned stanchions. This was normally a pretty easy job as the cows knew the routine and were anxious to get fed and rid themselves of the milk that in many cases was already streaming from their utters. There were forty-five to fifty assigned stanchions. We gave each cow a serving of hay, ensilage, and mixed grain/cotton seed/ oats, as prescribed on their charts. This diet helped ensure each cow received the proper nourishment for maximum health and milk production.

We proceeded to milk the cows, record the amount of milk they gave, and then led them back to their stanchions to finish their feed. After all the cows had been milked, we moved them to the upper pasture or back down to the lower pasture, depending upon where the grazing was best. In the winter, we bedded them down with fresh straw each day, as they remained in the barn.

The routine for checking traps was a bit more varied. We trapped in the early morning during the dead of winter. Even though Carolina winters are generally mild, there are days when ice forms on the creeks and ponds. We set traps along several streams up to three miles away from home. We trapped for muskrat, mink, and, on rare occasion, mad dog.

Introduction: Daily Life

After emptying the traps, we had to clean the pelts and stretch them for drying. The pelts were sold to Sears or Montgomery Wards. Each pelt brought from fifty-five cents to a high of three dollars and fifty cents. Those in charge of the boys and girls permitted a bit of slack as far as our daily routine was concerned. As long as we weren't causing trouble, did our chores in a good manner, and kept up with our studies, we could pursue our hobbies.

Trapping was one such hobby, and we were permitted to keep any money we earned. The same was true of picking and selling blackberries. This was a nice supplement to a teenager's income. We spent the money on electronic radio kits, blowguns, starter pistols, and chemicals for rockets.

If you did not have dairy duty, you were assigned to work on the truck farm where you planted vegetables, tended them, and later harvested and canned them. That was an all-spring/summer/fall job and was hard work. We canned hundreds of gallons of corn, tomatoes, green beans, lima beans, butter beans, green peas, black-eyed peas, and a combination of some of them. Our favorite was canned peaches. We often ate about as many as we canned. In addition to canning, we put up Irish and sweet potatoes, as well as turnips. We always had on hand a goodly supply of carrots, radishes, okra, cabbage, and lettuce. We all hated picking okra. It itched so badly.

Just as all the Home kids participated in the canning process, most of us participated in slaughtering and preparing meat from the hogs. As a special treat, we made a lot of cracklings. This consisted of the skin from the hogs, cut into pieces, deep-fried, and pressed into cakes. The cracklings were crisp and tasty, and nobody seemed to care that their nutritional value was questionable or downright bad for you by today's standards.

We could also be assigned to the big farm, which was responsible for all the grain, corn, ensilage, and hay for feeding the cattle and hogs. This was hard and hot work. Your day started at 7:30 a.m. and could go to as late as 8:00 p.m. depending on the crop we were harvesting and the weather.

Then there was the mill. We mixed our own feed for the cattle and hogs. This was a Saturday morning job and was assigned to those of us who were in need of some motivation – a different way of saying that we had been caught doing something wrong, failed to follow the rules, etc., during the week and were now "paying" for it. That usually meant that Gilmer and I, Bob Vickory, the Price boys, the Tuttles, and the Byrds were usually there. It was the worst job of all, terribly dusty. We ground the feed and then mixed it according to the directions we were provided by the dairy manager, Dad Shaver.

If you weren't assigned to one of the above job duties, you could be charged with kitchen, furnace, laundry, or delivery detail. Kitchen detail was an "up and at 'em" work schedule. Usually you were up at 5:30 each day. You were responsible for helping make toast and eggs for thirty or so kids as well as serve food and help clean up dishes. Furnace details required that you stoke the furnace each evening and add coal again during the day. It was busy, dusty work. Laundry detail involved helping load the laundry to be hauled by truck to our central laundry. In addition, if working on the laundry detail, you were responsible for sorting and handing out the clean laundry. Delivery detail was the "plum" job and was never held by a Murdock, a Price, a Byrd, or a Tuttle. We usually were at the dairy or Big Farm. On most Saturday afternoons, we could be found cleaning out the infamous "ditch." Approximately 200 yards long, the ditch was filled with the washdown from the milk room, which accumulated quite fast. It took several hours to pitch the holdings of the ditch up into the field.

We routinely got up at 6 o'clock each morning. Everyone showered, ate breakfast, consisting of either cereal, toast and jelly, or eggs, grits, and liver mush or bacon. After breakfast we would do one of the above assigned jobs. At approximately 8 o'clock we would head for school. Kindergarten through eighth grade was on campus, and grades nine through twelve took place at Richard J. Reynolds High School, about a mile walk off campus.

On occasion during the school day at Reynolds High School, they announced over the PA system that all Children's Home boys were excused to go get in potatoes, corn, hay, or whatever was being harvested at the time. For us, it meant "out of school for the day." None of us felt any embarrassment tied to that. We were proud to be from the Children's Home. We took a great deal of pride in doing our best at all times, and we were very competitive. For example, we had championship football, basketball, and baseball teams regularly.

After school, about 3:30 p.m., everyone would head for home. There were chores to do by kids of all ages, or if you participated in a sport there was practice, and afterwards supper. Our suppers consisted of simple country food, tasty and nourishing. Today it would be referred to as soul food. Usually it consisted of meat and three vegetables, including potatoes, turnip greens, peas or beans, with a desert in the form of peaches, applesauce, or, on rare occasion, pie and/or ice cream. We never went hungry.

After supper we did homework. If you had questions you could ask the Home Mother or one of the other kids. You could also ask Coach Gibson for help. There was very little time for anything else after your homework was completed, except preparing for the next day. Each person was responsible for ironing their own shirts and pants for school. (We never ironed our work clothes.) We were also responsible for keeping our rooms clean and orderly. There were two boys to a room, consisting of two dressers, a closet, and two single bunk beds. We had a central shower in each of the cottages, with toilet facilities. These facilities were always kept spotless. This applied to the girls' dorms as well as the cottages with the younger kids.

This routine was followed Monday through Friday, with Tuesday and/or Friday nights being open for participating in or attending one of the many sporting games in which we were involved. If you didn't go out for a sport, you were assigned to work. Needless to say, almost all the boys played football, with a few playing basketball and baseball. We also had great girls' basketball teams, which were very competitive.

In the off-season, we typically hung out in the recreation hall. Saturdays were the days that offered the greatest freedom. Ah … freedom … to roam the pastures, to work for extra money over in Buena Vista – a well-to-do neighborhood nearby – to pick blackberries, to see a movie downtown, to roam free!!!! We'll not mention stealing peaches, cakes, and watermelon at this time, other than to say that for years we thought the only good watermelon was a stolen one.

The summer, out-of-school months brought freedom from homework, but that was replaced with hoeing weeds, picking beans, tomatoes, corn, and countless other vegetables. The entire spring and early summer was spent planting and hoeing. It was also the season for getting in early crops such as radishes, onions, lettuce, carrots, and spinach. Summer saw harvests of straw and hay, and was the time for canning. The boys picked, and the girls and a few lucky boys canned. Gilmer and I rarely saw the cannery, except when we were sneaking up through the floor to "test" the canned peaches!

Our days were filled to the brim with things to do, most in a supervised fashion. However, there was still time to have great adventures. This book is about those times. Not every boy or girl was as adventuresome as we brothers or our close friends were … or perhaps they were and we didn't know it! Some adventures were best kept secret, which explains why we are now telling them for the very first time.

Richard J. Reynolds High School.

Flying Squirrels

"Our institution is called a Home, but we do not kid ourselves into believing that we can set up arrangements which will provide for normal home life. For one reason no home has twenty to thirty children in it, nor does a normal home provide eating tables for twenty to thirty children to gather around. We admit certain limitations in the matter of providing a substitute home for children. But we do not admit defeat at the matter of raising promising children. Our substitute home provides some mighty good features, which are more favorable for the upbringing of children than many private homes afford. In an institution such as ours there must be a morale on the part of staff workers and the children which tends towards making each one proud of the home in which he lives. Its work projects, its school activities, its athletic program, its social intercourse, its religious purposes and its idealism must be of a permeating and challenging type. We think we have some of all of this."

Blackberry Rain

Flying squirrels are quite unusual. Actually, they don't really fly; they simply glide, using the web of very soft skin that stretches out on each side of them from just back of their front feet to the front of their hind feet. They are very light and have large, dark eyes and are just the cutest things …unless you're Anna Brown.

One year I recovered a male baby flying squirrel from a fallen tree and raised it. He got quite large as he was well fed, but even a large flying squirrel is very light. Being nocturnal, he slept during the day – usually in a shoebox in the top of my closet. On this particular day, he had slipped into my shirt pocket.

Having to do extra chores at the dairy that morning, I was running late for school. In my haste, I showered quickly, with maybe three or four drops of water hitting me, toweled off, slipped on a change of clothes, hastily put on my shirt, grabbed my coat, and ran. I raced out the front entrance to the Home (past the sign that said: WE LOVE OUR CHILDREN. DRIVE CAREFULLY), took a shortcut across the field onto a large steel sewer pipe crossing the creek, and up the hill to Richard J. Reynolds High School. The pipe was still covered with morning dew and luckily I didn't slip. I guess if you are moving so fast that your feet don't actually touch the pipe, there is no problem.

By the time I got to school, homeroom was letting out and I was on my way to social studies and to the movie of the day. I sat down in my seat behind the lovely Anna Brown. A few minutes into the movie, most of the boys were asleep, including this one.

The next thing I remember was loud screaming that woke me with such a start that I kicked my shin against Anna's

Chapter 1: Flying Squirrels

desk chair, which was already on the move. All I could hear were kids screaming RAT, RAT, RAT, as Anna was lunging forward along with her desk chair. I didn't know whether to scream and run myself, as my mind couldn't quite grasp what was happening. What was the great panic? Then suddenly, just before the lights came back on, a flying squirrel hit me in the chest and scampered back into my shirt pocket. I immediately knew what had happened to cause all the commotion!

Apparently the lights had been off for several minutes, when Twit (my pet flying squirrel) decided it was time to come out and play. He jumped from me onto the back of Anna's head. Anna instantly came unglued, and screamed RAT! RAT!! RAT!!! She didn't bother getting properly out of her desk chair. She simply stood up with the desk chair still attached to her bottom and plowed through several students, not so much on her way somewhere as on her way away from where the RAT was.

Meanwhile the projector had been knocked over, and several of the schools largest, and up to this point perceived to be bravest, young men were rushing through the door, chivalry be damned, followed closely by the teacher (!!) and the rest of the class.

When the lights came back on, the room was in total disarray – desk chairs were turned over, books strewn about, and a faint stream of what looked like water on the floor led from the front of the room through the door and down the hall.

This single incident was responsible for several classes in the near vicinity panicking. Among the students running for dear life down the hall, I thought I even saw Calmadge Jones, a Home boy who avoided chaos and any kind of attention as often as possible.

I never let onto anything. So no one ever learned where the rat came from, or even if there was a rat. For me, the funniest part was listening to all the guys trying to come up with good excuses for why they were running.

The incident was soon forgotten by all but Anna Brown. I wouldn't be surprised to learn that she hasn't been to a movie since. I'll never forget seeing that pretty young lady with her desk chair still attached to her bottom, plowing through several other students on her way toward the teacher. Come to think of it, that "water" trail did lead from the front of the class where the teacher had been sitting at his desk …

Sliding Board

"Within the past few days two influential representatives of boards of trustees of other prominent North Carolina orphanages have called on us for information as to how 'we get so much done for so little outlay.' To each representative we have stated that we are not quite sure whether their opinion of us is complimentary. It was stated that there is such a thing as depriving children of certain necessities of life to which they should be entitled. Our challenge here at the Children's Home is not only to live within our income but to so use this income as to provide the best possible living conditions for our family. If it is a sin to waste, it would be doubly sinful to waste the charitable contributions of friends who want their money to be transplanted into Christian character. So the obligation of the use of our friends' money continually rests upon us with an emphasis we dare not trifle with."

Baby cottage.

Chapter 2: Sliding Board

There are times when ingenuity is required! It was a cold day by North Carolina standards, but Miss Carter, our Home Mother, had still allowed all the kids at baby cottage to go out and play. We were playing on the different yard toys and thought there might be a better and faster way to go down the sliding board. That's when we spotted a cardboard box. It looked just small enough to fit on the sliding board and large enough to hold one person.

Neither my brother Gilmer nor I or our friend Walter Jones wanted to try our hand at it, so we unanimously elected Sue Heart. Even at a young age Sue was bright. It took a bit of persuading to convince her to get in the box at the top of the slide, which to us looked like 100 feet high. But Sue finally fit herself into the box, and we started to push her.

This was the first (and certainly not the last!) time I was introduced to the euphemistic use of the word "oops." This was not a word one spoke lightly. It usually meant that something had gone wrong. And in this situation, this was indeed the case! Instead of Sue sliding down the board, she started end-over-end rolling down the slide in the card-board box. Each roll elicited a yell from Sue, and even many of the onlookers. Before Sue hit the ground, Walter and I, who had also been up on the stairs, were off and running into the crowd to be as inconspicuous as possible. Gilmer, on the other hand, was still standing at the top of the stairs to the slide, looking in utter amazement at Sue in her pathetic, unstoppable roll.

But it was too late! Miss Carter had spotted the tragic heap at the bottom of the sliding board as well as Gilmer, the culprit, at the top. She immediately ran over to Sue and verified that she was indeed still alive, though not the same person as she had been moments before the slide of her life began.

In a flash, Gilmer was marched off to stand in the corner. But after a few minutes, he motioned me over to take his place. Being identical twins had its benefits, as we could trade punishment and cut the ordeal in half. Little did anyone know … or so we thought.

At just the right moment, I darted over to take his place as he mingled into the rush of other games. Less than a minute had gone by when Miss Carter appeared next to me, paddle in hand, announcing, "Now I'm going to give you that spanking you deserve."

That was the end of our "trading places" routine. I think Sue finally forgave us, but it was probably years before she ever trusted a boy again. Sue, if you ever read this … Walter Jones put us up to it!!

CHAPTER 3:

Embarrassed

"We tell our children that the most correct estimation of the value of the Children's Home is determined by the character of our youngsters. We remind them that the Children's Home is not so much measured by our beautiful grounds and stately buildings, our big farming operations and athletic teams, but rather by the behavior of our boys and girls. Just how far this idea is transferred into the makeup of our youthful family is subject to gratification or doubt, depending on the trend of their doings."

(Top and bottom) Watermelon feast.

Chapter 3: Embarrassed

Tula Harrison, the Goddess of Threatened Punishment, was the sort of person every kid has had in his or her life at one time or other. The threat of all threats, "I'll put you in a sack and mop the floor with you," was taken seriously when directed toward you or a group of your buddies. She was a large boned (huge) woman with a menacing look. Looking back, she was a truly positive influence on us all, and according to the girls, was a wonderful person.

There are some things that boys under twelve just don't do. It is an unwritten law that boys that age do not hug girls, are never seen in or near a girls' bathroom, and never ever do anything that would bring shame on their buddies, or, at the risk of offending Tula Harrison, bring embarrassment upon the Home Mothers.

That may all be true unless you are Tinker Rouse, "Tink" for short. Tink didn't adhere to any code of conduct, much less one that involved girls or etiquette. At that age, Tink thought girls didn't exist; he had no clue of proper etiquette, or improper etiquette for that matter.

It was Sponsor Day at the Home. Each church group sponsoring one of the boys or girls from the Home was invited to visit and meet the sponsored boy or girl in his or her natural setting – sounds like a zoo, I know. The truth is, there were days when this metaphor was not far off! The event gave the sponsors an opportunity to see the cottages and meet the Home Mothers.

Days were spent preparing for this special event. Care was taken to ensure that the cottages were clean and the campus was neat and orderly. Each boy and girl was reminded to put his or her "best foot forward." (I never understood that saying. For years, I thought most people were born with a gimp foot and could only show their good one. But then again, I often pondered the song "I wonder who's kissing her now?" Quite honestly, I didn't know what a "now" was, and at eleven years old, I was way, way too embarrassed to ask …)

Routinely, several of us boys decided that since we didn't have to work on the farm that day, we'd sneak off to pick blackberries. This was a favorite pastime, as it allowed us to venture beyond the campus into the unknown. Usually that was just over the hill of the upper pasture near an old white church. Most of the Home boys knew that was where Paula Ray was buried. Paula Ray, a young girl from the Home, had died many years earlier. Word was that if you walked around her grave three times and said, "Paula Ray, Paula Ray, what are you doing?" she would answer, "Nothing." At least that's what we were told, but none of us ever felt the need to test our bravery by doing it … or expose a lack thereof.

On this day, we had a particularly good berry-picking adventure. Tink had picked up a sizable box at the gully (the Children's Home dump site), and we had it completely full in no time. Having eaten our fill, and the hot noonday sun starting to take its toll, we decided it was time we got back. As we approached the football field, we noticed that all the sponsors and many of the boys and girls were enjoying a picnic-style lunch. All we could think of was Miss Holland's fried chicken and potato salad, so we hastened our pace.

Tink Rouse was leading the pack of shirtless, tanned boys as we came onto the field, still busy munching on blackberries from the box we had filled. As we got closer, we suddenly noticed that the crowd was getting quieter and quieter. Just then, from out of nowhere, came Tula Harrison,

Chapter 3: Embarrassed

Goddess of Threatened Punishment ... Snatch!! ... Whap!! ... The box of blackberries was gone, and an instant knot was visited upon poor Tink's head. The rest of us immediately distanced ourselves from Tink, as was our way. If one boy got into trouble, the rest of us managed to become invisible, very quickly. Some would call us cowards ... they would be right ... but it was a way of life.

A moment or two passed before the silence was broken with Coach Clary announcing that they were going to cut the watermelon. It was customary to line up about twenty of the South's favorite summer refreshment – watermelon – on the football field bleachers to be enjoyed as a snack, hors d'oeuvres, lunch, dinner, or dessert. Regardless of what you call it, it was always a special treat.

It wasn't until later that we learned that the blackberries weren't confiscated because we weren't allowed to have them. They were confiscated because the box they were in was a Kotex box. So Tink was seen eating out of a Kotex box by all the sponsors – an indignation for any boy, for sure, but far worse for establishing poor demeanor for good Christian children. But then Tink wasn't into demeanor, and nor were we.

Normally it would be a while before any boy lived down this kind of embarrassing incident, but shortly afterwards we were in the thick of it again.

Boys' cottage – Tise 1 and Tise 2.

CHAPTER 4:

Poisoned

"We have a worry clinic. This clinic has a weekly session and is subject to convening on call. Into this clinic come the youngsters who need a diagnosis and along with him comes the Home Mother who sometimes feels that the youngster needs more than a diagnosis. Our worry clinics may not solve everything but they do give a lift to the lagging spirits of those who are called in. We have noted that when the worry is transferred from the director to the one directed the tendency is to have no worry."

Blackberry Rain

Aswimming hole was something to be revered. There was hardly ever a day in the fields, from May through the middle of September, that didn't warrant a chance to hit a swimming hole. Sometimes it was in the bottoms at the river and many other times it was in a pond. It may even have been an abandoned pool. If you went to a swimming hole, rules applied. Rule number 2 was "Don't tell."

It was a particularly hot day in early May. Rumor had reached us about a house owned by Richard J. Reynolds, of tobacco fame, and it had a swimming pool some way past the main house, out of both sight and earshot. This was much too tempting to pass up, so several of us decided to sneak off to find this forbidden pool. As I recall, with some questionable remembrance, there were Walter Jones, Wilbur Brown, Grady Lord, Tink Rouse, Sam Vickory, Gilmer, and I.

Our directions were somewhat sketchy, but we started out toward what we thought was the right location. On the way, we had to pass through two pond/swamp areas full of lilies, frogs, and water moccasins. We worked our way gingerly on the shallow edges, ever watchful of the snakes … there were lots of them.

Finally, we came within sight of the pool. It was filled with water but had not yet been cleaned out for the summer season. There was a diving board at one end and a pool house that appeared to be locked at the other.

There was absolutely no hesitation. Home boys were fiercely competitive, so very soon, seven huge splashes could be heard at the exactly the same time. If you have ever seen a Superman movie, you have an idea of how fast we shucked

Chapter 4: Poisoned

our clothes and hit the water. It all started about fifty feet from the pool. Shirts, pants, underwear. It was a blur.

After about twenty minutes of frenzied play, and many gulps of pool water, we started to settle down and look around. We couldn't hear anyone and could not see the house up the winding path for some large magnolias, rhododendrons, and pine trees.

Only then we noticed that the pool water was somewhat green looking. In fact, there was quite a bit of algae. Upon closer examination, it appeared that the pool house was abandoned. Though locked, the door was off its hinges and a side window was broken. Also, further inspection revealed that the pool itself appeared abandoned as the walk around it was cracked in several places.

Amidst all these discoveries what sounded like a gag from eating a molded cake from a Merrita Bread pigpen run welled up from Grady, those occasional feasts when we sneaked stale bread and cakes intended as pig feed. We all looked at him the exact same time … ever vigilant of getting caught. Grady appeared to be trying to puke and spit at the same time. His eyes were bulging out, and he was only able to desperately point to the skimmer pocket on the side of the pool. What ensued after that could be likened to seeing six kids who had just witnessed a sideshow act of a man biting the head off a live chicken. Everybody was spitting, hawking up anything they could and trying frantically to puke.

There in the skimmer was the largest dead, swollen rat any of us had ever seen. All any of us could think of was that it was diseased, that it had maggots crawling out of it, that it was dead from drinking poisoned water, or that a water moccasin had gotten it, and that we were all going to die …

if not from the disease, the poison, the imaginary maggots, the water moccasin, at least from the sheer thought of it.

After several minutes of breathless eternity, we were able to start breathing again. Needless to say, no one was going back into that pool. Then, as reality began to set in, we remembered Rule Number 1: "Don't get caught."

That's when we heard a dog barking. It sounded like a large dog. The sound kept getting closer and closer. The closer it got, the louder it got ... and the bigger it got. By now, in everyone's mind it was enormous, and no doubt mad and foaming at the mouth.

As if all this wasn't bad enough, we suddenly remembered that we were all buck-naked and that our clothes were strewn along the way in the direction from which we came. Again, a blur of activity, this time with a different emotion and much greater sense of urgency ... utter fear. We were grabbing for our clothes and running at the same time.

By the time we stopped running, we were over half way back home. We must have set a record for the two-mile sprint. We stopped in a grove of familiar pines and caught our breath. Only then could we start to feel at ease. Nevertheless, to be safe, we were still spitting.

As the adrenalin subsided, we started to reflect on what had happened. Then we started to laugh. We laughed so hard it hurt. Looking back, we couldn't remember leaving the pool area ... one microsecond we were there, the next we were not. In fact, we don't know how we were able to get dressed in a flat-out "fear-for-your-life run." None of us remember crossing back over the lily ponds. I vaguely recall thinking at the time that Tink Rouse's feet never went

Chapter 4: Poisoned

under the water as he flew past us, with what appeared to be a snake clinging to his trouser leg. All we did know was that we survived and hadn't gotten caught or …

Miss Little was in charge of Tise 1 at the time, and Miss Reynolds was in charge of Tise 2. Tise 1 and Tise 2 were separate cottages but located in the same building. It was two stories high with a large full basement and housed thirty or so boys on each side. About a week later, we were feeling pretty confident that all was well and started to relax again, with the pool adventure all but forgotten, but, sure enough, Wilbur Brown was suddenly called in from Tise 1 and I was called in from Tise 2. Immediately, we were confronted by Miss Reynolds, Miss Little, and Tula Harrelson, who were staring at us as though they knew a secret and we were about to find out what it was.

In our haste to run from the mad dog, Wilbur had grabbed my underwear and I had grabbed his by mistake. At the Home, your name was on everything you owned. Since our laundry was washed and sorted separately by cottage, the great underwear mix-up was discovered. Before all was said and done, each of the seven of us was pulled in for interrogation. It appears that we had been seen together that Saturday.

No one knows how the pieces were all put together, but before it was over, the truth was out. We were busted. No doubt a part of the "fessing-up" came under the threat of Tula Harrison, Goddess of Threatened Punishment, putting us in a sack and mopping up the floor with us. I don't know if that ever had happened to any of the kids, but it sure was a threat to be taken seriously.

Blackberry Rain

As I recall, we were referred to Paul Booze, the farm manager, with reparation to be paid on the truck farm. We were not allowed to talk to each other for a couple of weeks and had to help plant.

Those were magic times with many friends. Little did we know how much we would come to value this "slice of heaven" for the rest of our lives. These great adventures are as fresh in our minds today as if they had happened yesterday. The world we lived in consisted of a beautiful campus – it had order, purpose, and held great promise. These were simple times for us kids with lots of laughter, surrounded by loving, caring adults.

CHAPTER 5:

'Til the Cows Come Home

"As the family here at the Children's Home has increased, the dairy production has increased, the minimum production now being 150 gallons per day. At times a record of over two hundred gallons per day has been made. The herd now measures 130, counting the Hereford steers, which are fattened for beef. This herd ranges over one hundred acres of improved pasture land for about seven months in the year, making the cost of up-keep of the herd much less than it would otherwise be."

Milking cows.

Chapter 5: 'Till the Cows Come Home

One thing is certain when you grow up on a dairy farm. You will milk cows twice a day, every day of the year.

At the Children's Home we did just that. Usually, we ran two shifts and alternated between the 3 a.m. milking and the 3 p.m. milking. The 3 a.m. milking was particularly challenging, because it was always dark when you started. In fact, it could be downright spooky.

In this case, it was an especially hot, foggy morning in June. You could barely see five or six feet in front of you. Jerry Murdock was particularly eager this morning, because he was going to sneak out early and try to scare Johnny Tuttle, Robert Davidson, and Roy Benge.

Each morning, the cows had to be herded up from the lower barn and lot to the milk barn. All the crew participated in this effort. This was where the event was to take place. Jerry had stealthily made his way into the lower lot and positioned himself among the cows. This was not a simple task because you couldn't see the fresh cow pies. You could only feel along with your bare feet, a grave concern, considering that these were not small Jersey or Guernsey milk cows but the larger Holsteins, who made larger cow pies.

Jerry's plan was to jump up yelling to scare the bejeezus out of the other boys. It was going to be great! He could almost see the fear in their eyes, the cold sweat on their foreheads, and feel the terror in their hearts. Just thinking about it, he had to choke back an impulse to burst out laughing.

As Jerry heard the lower lot gate swing open, he stood up from the crouched position he had assumed earlier ... and

Dairy barns on the property.

just then the absolute unbelievable happened. Sally, the largest cow we had at the time, weighing over a billion pounds (at least that's what it felt like at that moment) got startled and stepped back and right onto Jerry's bare foot.

What ensued was not your ordinary yell. This was a yell of incredible pain … of a billion-pound cow standing on his foot. It was a scream from the dark fog of the lower lot that chilled you to the bone and raised the hair on the back of your neck. The others instinctively knew that somebody or something was dying, and from the sound of it, being eaten alive!

At that time, the "all for one and one for all" creed legendary throughout the Home family went right out the window. Courage and fortitude vanished instantly. No one even dared to look at each other to see what they were going to do. It was every man for himself, as they raced hell bent for leather toward the cottages, with a herd of Holsteins following them in a stampede. They could still hear the agonizing screams of pain but knew whatever had caused this was very close behind them and nobody was stopping to look back.

Word has it that when the cows finally came home that morning, Dad Shaver milked them. He never did get the whole story until years later. To this day, Jerry still carries a scar on his foot, and Johnny Tuttle still is afraid of the fog.

Gilmer and Graham's class photo.

CHAPTER 6

Divine Intervention

"We have the feeling that our Children's Home staff members are doing a grand job. If there ever was a time some of our staff members were not happy in their work, it can be truly said such does not now prevail here with us. This happy situation offers our children fine instances of good leadership. It seems that the day children would have a dread of living here has passed away. Many instances of loving devotion towards the children are now listed among our adult leadership. If at times somebody was reported as having told somebody else about a little of nothing, that day is not now with us."

Blackberry Rain

Saturday was usually a great day for us kids at the Children's Home. This was the day when we, as teenagers, were given the opportunity to expand our horizons. The one thing the Children's Home staff sought to do was to instill respect for others and the value of hard work, and to teach Christian values. I have to admit that my brothers and I were a challenge for the staff and continually stretched their patience, but they never gave up on us, and kept encouraging us to grow into responsible adults.

Saturday was a perfect day for going to the movies, for example. With a Children's Home pass and ten cents, we could see any movie we wanted to see at either of the two downtown theaters. Saturday morning they usually showed the sequels to *Tarzan* and *Roy Rogers*, preceded by a broadcast of world news.

The trip to the movie could be an adventure in itself, as it was this particular Saturday. Curtis Cort and I were heading downtown … or uptown. I was never sure of which was which, but I think it had something to do with whether town was on a hill and you were above it or below it. Those were things too difficult for us kids to understand, so we left it to the adults. At any rate, we were on our way to the movie and had planned several stops along the way.

The first stop was the feed store to see what type of critters they had. Usually they had baby rabbits and chicks, and on occasion they had quail and wild turkeys. On Saturdays, this was a good place to get a firsthand look at a lot of farm folk and listen to their tales.

Our second stop was the Planters Peanut Store to buy some roasted peanuts and then on to Bocock Strouds, a local gentlemen's clothing store. A fellow at Bocock Strouds named Bill was not only an accomplished tailor but also a great storyteller, spinning a yarn or two as he tailored suits. To make matters even better, he also had chocolates for us. Occasionally, his older son would join us, but his wife always warned us not to believe Bill's stories.

The final stop was the movie theater itself. We would load up on popcorn and drinks, using money we had stashed from doing chores off campus or from selling blackberries.

Ray Bird, one of our Home brothers, always said that he could go into any movie theater and spot a Children's Home boy by the back of his head. That's the price we paid for free haircuts! At regular intervals, we piled into the Children's Home bus for a ride uptown to the barber college. What young lad would want to miss the opportunity to have his hair cut by a barber student! Let me put it this way. In addition to getting a goodly supply of hair down your back, you would most likely end up in a chair back at the Home to get things straightened out by your Home Mother. Free haircuts came with gaps and notches. It was sometimes a pitiful sight.

There were a couple of ways to get to town. You could follow the main road off the campus south and up the hill toward Centenary Methodist Church; you could cut up the hill toward our English teacher's house, Miss Rhodes, or you could walk along the railroad tracks into town and cut over to the feed store. The route along the railroad tracks took longer because there was a long bridge to cross. There was also a long curve just before the bridge, both ways, and you could not see a train coming either way until it was nearly up on you. We had to wait and listen for a train and build up the nerve to cross. That also took time, sometimes a long time.

Nevertheless, we chose the railroad track route this Saturday. As we neared the tracks, we were already thinking about the train. There was something else we were thinking about and that was the Lander gang. They were four of the meanest kids we knew living outside the campus in a poor area of town called Chatham that we had to pass through. Their leader was Hoyt Lander. The folks in Chatham were for the most part mill workers. Having delivered papers to many of them, I knew most of them to be kind and hard working. But the Lander gang was made up of misfits, and they were meaner than junkyard dogs. They were always spoiling for a fight but were afraid to take on a Home boy because they knew it wasn't just one or two boys they would be dealing with. They would have to take on twenty or thirty.

It took us about half an hour to reach the train bridge over Peters Creek. First we stood as still as we could, listening intently. We placed our ears next to the rail. We could hear nothing. We waited a few minutes and tried to remember the time of day the trains came down the tracks. This seemed to be a good time to cross, so off we went at a brisk pace along the edge of the bridge.

We tried not to look down, forcing ourselves to look straight ahead. The height of the bridge wasn't that great. It was around forty feet in the center of the creek, and the creek was about six feet deep at that point. The worst thing that could happen if you fell was that you would get drenched. That's if you hit the creek. If you hit the sides or the bank that would mean red Carolina mud ... and lots of it.

We were relieved that, once again, we had made it across with no train, but we were barely ready to move on toward the feed store, when we heard a sound immediately behind us that caused us to nearly jump out of our skin. It was an incredibly loud train whistle. A passenger train had crept up on us! Curtis and I both jumped away from the tracks and ran up the bank faster than a speeding bullet. We thought we were dead.

After the six-car train passed, we started to breathe again, amazed at how it had appeared out of nowhere. Again, it embedded in our minds the reason why we had to be cautious crossing the bridge.

We finally made it to the feed store, where we listened to the farmers talk about the war, new tractors, new combines, and a new corn seed that grew ears of corn that tasted so sweet it was like eating sugar. One of the farmers was talking about a Thermos bottle he had just bought; the sales person told him that it would keep cold things cold and hot things hot. When asked what he had in his Thermos that day, he answered, "soup and popsicles."

We missed Bill, our tailor friend at Bocock Strouds, who had taken the day off, but we did make it to the peanut store. The peanuts were hot and delicious. We had saved some for the movie, but they went fast as we met up with several of the other Home gang.

After the movie let out, we started talking to the other Home boys and girls about the fastest way back to the campus. We decided we would race and see which way was the fastest, follow the road back through town or the railroad tracks. Curtis decided to walk with the other kids as he had enough of the train tracks. Gilmer and Walter said they would walk with me back down the tracks.

Off we went. Gilmer, Walter, and I passed the feed store and started down the tracks heading west. I told them about

the Thermos, and Walter wanted to know how it could tell
to keep things hot or to keep things cold. That was a bit
over our heads, so we changed the subject. Up ahead of
us we could see a large thunderhead approaching. A nice
breeze had picked up.

We were laughing about the train incident Curtis and I
had earlier in the day. We were once again at the bridge.
This time we were heading in the direction of the train
and felt a bit better about that (I only remember the train
going in one direction, from west to east). We went through
the routine of listening for the train, and once again heard
nothing. We were about a third of the way across when who
should appear at the other end of the bridge but the Lander
gang. They looked like they were spoiling for a fight and
started calling us names as we walked toward them. They
shouted that they weren't going to let us by and started to
head across the bridge toward us.

Just then we heard that dreaded sound … a train whistle.
The only problem was that it was behind us. That's right, the
train was going east to west and that meant we were trapped
with only two ways to go. We either had to jump into the
creek below or fight our way through the Lander gang. We
elected to keep going straight at them. Again we heard the
train whistle, now much closer. We started to run, figuring
our momentum would help increase our size, as those boys
were each bigger than us. Gilmer squeezed into the lead, with
Walter and me within inches of him.

Then the unexpected happened. Or rather, it was not just
unexpected; it was divine intervention! A tremendous bolt
of lightning struck right behind the Lander gang, and an
enormous thunderclap deafened us all. Gilmer, Walter,
and I slid to a stop, our hearts pounding. Then in utter

amazement, we watched the Lander gang literally fly off the bridge, headlong into the creek. With no time to spare, we bolted to the other side of the bridge and jumped to the bank just as a three-locomotive freight train passed us going at least fifty miles an hour. I presume it was blowing its whistle when it went by but none of us heard it!

As we stood up, we looked down in the creek some eighty feet away and a bit downstream. The four members of the Lander gang were just getting to the bank, all looking like drenched rats, soaked from head to toe and covered in mud. They had landed in the mud at the edge of the creek and their momentum had carried them into the six-foot deep water. They weren't saying a word. We knew we wouldn't have to worry about them now. The fear of God had just been pounded into them.

Even with the excitement of the train, the Lander gang, and the lightning, we still remembered that we had a race to run, so off we went. We were racing the other Home kids, but we were also racing the rain that was sure to be coming any minute. As we reached the back entrance to the campus, Curtis and the others were just reaching it as well. It was a tie, but we weren't going to debate it. We all headed directly toward our cottages.

The girls barely made it inside as the torrential rain hit. But Curtis, Gilmer, Walter, a couple of the other boys, and I just started walking. We were soaking up every drop of rain we could. We told everyone the story and stopped along the way to laugh. Here was the Lander gang getting literally exploded off the bridge by lightening. We must have had a guardian angel watching over us. We never again had an encounter with those boys. No one did.

Blackberry Rain

When Walter, Curtis, Gilmer, and I went back to the train bridge, we couldn't figure out why lightening had struck where it did. There were no trees of any size. There were no steel signs. It simply happened. I can only believe the boys in the Lander gang changed their ways that day after getting the message.

CHAPTER 7:

Peaches

"We do not crowd our children with religious treatises or ecclesiastical dogma. Religion with us is largely a matter of properly motivated behavior. Many of our children do not know that they have been "born again" since their borning has been over such a long period of processing as to not have any outstanding eventful happening. This status of affairs used to bother us quite a lot in our intellectual thinking. We have come to be more interested in their fairness of action, diligence of purpose, and fervency of spiritual devotion to Christian ideals."

Girls canning peaches.

Chapter 7: Peaches

Afterall these years, I can still hear Mrs. Smith screaming with her mouth full of food and see her running toward the stairs. In the process, chairs and tables were parting in the dining room as if she was running from the devil himself.

It was a few days before summer vacation was to begin. Everyone was excited at the prospect of going away for the three-week break as was customary every August. Away from the dairy and milking twice a day, away from the farm and hoeing those endless rows of corn, away from throwing hay bales, away from grinding feed in the mill, away from the main dining hall, and away from the central laundry.

Planning for our "piece of cake adventure," in this case, "can of peaches adventure" had taken place several days before. The other person involved, W. H. (a.k.a. Winfred Hammer), and I planned to leave a window to the cafeteria unlocked the day we had kitchen duty, which was Tuesday. We knew that the next day was the day that Miss Smith, who was in charge of the cafeteria, was off, and that she would not be around.

Things were working out quite well. We got the window unlocked and left the pantry door unlocked. We also set out a gallon of peaches, a plain gallon can marked with two strokes of yellow paint, in the pantry within easy reach. At the Home, we canned our own fruits and vegetables, marking the top of the gallon can with the color of the fruit or vegetable it contained. Red for tomatoes, green for beans, red and green for lima beans and tomatoes, double yellow for peaches, and a single yellow line for corn.

It was about 7 p.m. on the appointed day, and the kitchen was closed. Everyone was doing his or her thing on this hot early-August evening. Winfred and I met up and headed for the kitchen window. We cautiously looked around and made our way over to the window, opened it, and quickly crawled inside. We listened very carefully. The only thing we could hear was our hearts beating wildly. We hurried to the pantry, opened the door, and darted inside. We had barely closed the pantry door when we heard a dreaded sound ... a key in the door at the other end of the dining room from the stairs leading to the living quarters. I grabbed the peaches and dove under a large meat-cutting table. Winfred closed the pantry door behind him on his way past me and disappeared.

As we learned later, Mrs. Smith had come back early from her day off and was walking through the cafeteria and into the kitchen. You could tell it was her by the sound of her walking, the swishing of her rolled-down nylon hose rubbing together; besides, I could see her white shoes. She went to the refrigerator and got the makings for a sandwich, picked up a plate, and came over to the table I was hiding under. To this day I do not understand why she didn't hear my heart beating. Lord knows it about deafened me. Worse yet, where was Winfred?

Lying breathless under the table, only inches from Mrs. Smith's shoes, all I could think: Here goes the vacation, here comes three weeks in the ditch, and a sound talking to and whopping with the famous Coach Clary paddle (it had holes in it to give it less wind resistance). My life as I knew it was over.

In the meantime, Mrs. Smith fixed her sandwich, got some milk, and commenced eating right there over me. After what felt like an eternity, she finally started to leave. But where in God's name was Winfred?

Mrs. Smith finally took the last bite of her sandwich and walked over to the large commercial-style dishwasher. She placed her glass and plate on the dishwasher tray and hit the start button. Just as she began to push the tray through the canvas strips and into the dishwasher, a blood-curdling scream sounded from the dishwasher. That's right ... Winfred had hidden in the dishwasher. The sudden shock of cold water and the fact that his heart was already in his mouth made it impossible for him to hold back a high-pitched, ear-shattering scream.

But Winfred wasn't the only one who freaked out. Mrs. Smith came totally unglued. She was so scared that she ran blindly the full length of the kitchen, dining room, and up the stairs to her room screaming the whole way, chairs and tables flying in every direction in her wake.

Not missing a beat, Winfred flew out the other side of the dishwasher, and the two of us bolted out the window. Neither of us was first, and neither of us was last. We looked like one kid coming through that window. We immediately hid the peaches and snuck in the back door so Winfred could change clothes and dry his hair. Then off we went to mingle in the crowd.

But things didn't end there. About twenty minutes later, everybody was summoned to the line-up, a standard Home investigative method used to solve transgressions and other mysteries around campus.

No one admitted anything and no one was ever caught. In true Children's Home fashion, no one "fessed up." Even though we escaped "unscathed," it was a bitter-sweet victory: When we went back to get the peaches we had hidden, they were gone! To this day we don't know who got them and we weren't asking.

Home Mothers.

CHAPTER 8:

The Silk Purse

"We here at the Children's Home are looking for results. We are tremendously interested in attitudes guaranteeing desired results. We have a minimum amount of supervision. We have a maximum amount of personal direction. With us the most important persons in the development of character are our Home Mothers. Their importance and their prerogatives are not trampled on. They are supported and encouraged to a marked extent. Frequent conferences enable them and us to work together with clear avenues of service in mind. The same is true with our department heads. Thus we get along without any great amount of centralized direction and regulation."

Blackberry Rain

It was a typical hot summer Saturday in the North Carolina Great Smokey Mountain foothills. The winding country roads were refreshed with a light breeze and a recent morning rain. Noon was fast approaching, and our brother Jim was eagerly waiting for a car that he expected would be coming down the country road any minute. It was all he, our older brother Vance, and his two buddies could do to hold back the laughter at the mere thought of what was lying ahead.

June and Robert Lotharp, two local black kids, were the greatest pals anyone could have. And to top it off, their mom was a terrific cook and nurse. Her home remedies saved us many times when we had been stung by wasps or bitten by snakes. We even were able to survive stepping on rusty nails due to her magic potions. Our vacations away from the Home always included fun with them. Our older brothers were their family's good friends as well.

Robert and June's older brothers and a couple of their friends had been invited to take a ride in a car. This was a special treat, as few of our folks or their friends could afford a car in those days. There were six of them in the car … no air conditioning, except speed and four open windows.

As they zipped along at speeds reaching forty miles per hour, they turned down the road where they knew Vance and Jim would be waiting for them. It was going to be great … an opportunity to show off.

From their hiding place above the edge of the road, Jim, Vance, and their two friends, Buck and Clyde, were peering at the place in the road where they had just deposited a medium-sized silk purse.

Chapter 8: The Silk Purse

Over the hill soon came the long-awaited car. You could hear the laughter and excitement coming from the car. But … zoom … they went right past the purse! Vance muttered something and Jim murmured his disappointment, but suddenly the car slid to a stop, kicking up a large cloud of dust on the dirt road. It started to back up at a high rate of speed and came to a stop right next to the purse. Right then, the back door opened, and a large black hand reached out, grabbed the purse, slammed the door, and off they went again.

No one in the car was going to miss his share of what was in the purse. Those in front were reaching back as those in back were trying to wrestle the purse open. It was going to be the find of the century, and everyone was going to share in it, and that was firm.

As those on the bank observed, with deafening silence, the car speeding away, it was as if time stood still. But the car had gone no more than fifty feet when it looked as if an explosion had occurred, and everything was happening in slow motion. All four doors of the car burst open at the same time. Bodies were hurling themselves out on both sides. The driver had one foot on the brake, was trying to steer with one hand, and was hobbling alongside the car with the other foot. Fear and panic was the order of the day.

In what was to be a secret kept throughout their lives was the truth behind the world's greatest practical joke. Jim and Vance were just back from the war, and they had agreed to meet up with Robert and June's brothers and take turns driving the car. Vance, Jim, Buck, and Clyde were on their way to the meeting place along the road when they happened upon an empty silk purse. It was as if an inspiration hit all four of them simultaneously.

Blackberry Rain

The first to open the purse was Leroy, who was sitting in the middle of the back seat. His eyes got as wide as paper plates as he lunged out the right-side back door without hardly touching Cletus, who was sitting next to him. What was left lying in the seat was the largest, hottest, meanest blacksnake anyone had ever seen – a full six feet long!

Screams of laughter louder than anyone had ever heard before came from the guys on the hill. No one knows if the guys in the car screamed, because no one could hear them. All Vance and company could remember were six guys running through the woods and an empty car slowly rolling to a stop in the middle of the dirt road.

Our brother told us this story some years ago. To this day, no one has ever repeated it. Vance, Jim, Buck, and Clyde have since passed on as has everybody else in the car. He told me that they laughed four years of war away that day.

Chapter 9:

A Rat in the Closet

"In a family as large as ours there are some children who give us a great deal of concern. In every cottage there is one or more youngsters who keep the Home Mother from settling down too much in ease and comfort. We sometimes tell the Home Mothers that these youngsters are there to develop their personalities and resourcefulness. At any rate, they are there and it is easier to talk about them than it is to deal with them."

Wren Cottage for Boys (top) and Neal Cottage for Boys (bottom).

Chapter 9: A Rat in the Closet

When the boys at the Home got older, they gained certain privileges, and some customary routines were no longer required. Among the latter, older boys were not required to shower as a group. After soaping up, the younger kids had to face the Home Mother with their hands over their head and turn around. This inspection, which ensured your "outer cleanliness," continued until you were out of Tise 2, around the age of 12. Pop Woosley, who brought the wrath of Cain down on each and every one of us boys and girls every Sunday, ensured our "inner cleanliness."

One of the privileges we gained was moving to different rooms. You moved from a thirty-plus room to a room for two. The two-to-a-room was really special because it meant fewer disturbances and more privacy. Privacy privileges were permitted unless you did something to discourage them. Privacy included being able to leave your door closed, staying up past nine o'clock at night, listening to a radio, and not having your room searched for neatness or questionable items … such as pets.

From the time I was in Norfleet at about age 14, I kept and raised baby squirrels, usually left homeless by a tree limb breaking during a storm.

In high school I had a squirrel that was quite large, having raised it from a baby. It slept in a coat pocket on my side of the closet when it wasn't outside. One fateful day our Home Mother was testing our honesty regarding privacy privileges. She rummaged through closets and came to our room and our closet. She reached her hand into my jacket pocket and my squirrel, not recognizing the scent on her hand, bit as hard as he could. In fact, as squirrels do, he bit her three times in rapid succession … chomp, chomp, chomp!

I can only imagine the Home Mother's scream and sheer terror. As she frantically pulled her hand back with a squirrel clinging to it, she didn't recognize it as a squirrel but ran down the hall screaming, "RAT, a VERY LARGE RAT!" leaving a trail of blood all the way to her room at the other end of the building.

Later in the day when I returned to the house, I saw the blood on the floor and followed the trail back to my room. The door was open, the closet door was off its hinge, a chair was turned over, the lamp was knocked on the floor, alongside my coat, which had been pulled off the hanger – all signs that someone had been in a mighty hurry.

I quickly surmised that Rufus, my pet squirrel, had been the focus of this activity. He normally stayed on a shelf at the top of my closet, but he wasn't there. After some searching, I finally found him in a coat pocket.

I immediately cleaned up all signs of squirrel such as nuts and water and put Rufus outside, where he stayed most of the time anyway. Then I closed the window screen so he couldn't get back in should there be an inspection. Sure enough, not an hour had gone by before Mr. Simpson and Eddie Newsome, two of the staff, appeared to deal with the RAT. Naturally, we denied everything.

The bandage on our Home Mother's finger was large. I never questioned why she was sneaking into our room, and she pretty much let go of the rat issue. I think each boy enjoyed an increased level of privacy from that point on, which explains why Walter Whiteing, another Home boy, was able to hide a shotgun under his mattress.

CHAPTER 10:
Squirrel Hunting

"Any home so run as to cause an inferiority complex in the lives of its children should bestir itself for changing such a condition. Children torn away from their normal homes should not be further penalized by having to live in a second rate institution, particularly when such an institution can be a first rate one. We have the feeling that our Methodist people desire to provide for their dependent children a home in which both the children and they may have a definite pride."

Campus School.

Chapter 10: Squirrel Hunting

The Children's Home boys and girls were renowned for their ingenuity, among other worldly traits, such as becoming invisible when sneaking out. The Home Mothers countered by being able to see invisible people, as we personally witnessed on many occasions.

The boys were known for raising squirrels, both grey and flying squirrels. In addition we were famous for making slingshots. The best ones were made from the limb forks of a dogwood tree. The idea was to bend them just right so they formed a U shape and then wrap wire around the prongs to hold them in place and bake them in foil in a fire. This would harden them and make them nearly unbreakable. We used old car tire inner tubes for the rubber and made the pockets out of leather. This process was passed to me from Jim McDay. Marbles were our favorite ammo.

Just about every Home boy had a slingshot. Always hidden. When the occasion presented itself, such as a spontaneous rabbit or squirrel hunt, out came the slingshots. Each year, Coach Gibson volunteered to take the boys on a Thanksgiving rabbit hunt, which was a much-anticipated event. We usually ended up shooting each other with the slingshot or stomping each other's feet in pursuit of rabbits. They always got away, but it sure was a lot of fun. I'll never forget the knot on Bill Dolbys' head left by a marble fired from Walter Green's slingshot. Just as he was firing, he was whacked by a branch coming back from the guy in front of him. I never did tell anyone where I was at that moment …

A late-fall Saturday, we were at the pavilion, a large area with two picnic shelters and several benches. We noticed a couple of boys trying to shoot a squirrel out of a very tall tulip poplar tree behind Miss Sifford's cottage, the Haynes cottage. At the time it seemed to be 100 feet tall, but, in reality, it was more like sixty feet. In the very top was a large grey squirrel. No one could hit it. It kept moving behind limbs.

Soon about fifteen of us were surrounding the tree. The difficulty was that as we kept missing the squirrel, the ricochets were zinging down on the boys on the opposite side of the tree. We were causing such a ruckus that Coach Clary was finally summoned.

Unfortunately, Walter Whiteing was not aware of this. Walter had a shotgun hidden under his bed. While none of us had noticed, he ran in, grabbed the gun, and came out the back door. All of a sudden there was a deafening blast, just as Clary was nearing the front of the building.

By the time Coach Clary ran around to the back, about 100 feet, there was not a single soul in sight. The only thing was the resounding echo and a wisp of smoke from the shotgun. Fifteen or so boys had melted away as if they had stepped through a doorway into thin air.

Because Coach didn't find a body, of squirrel or boy, he was probably grateful, and let the moment pass. I don't recall if Walter was caught, but I am sure the shotgun disappeared forever. Luck like that just didn't get visited down on us too often.

CHAPTER 11:

The Law of Gravity

"Now is the time for action. The need for giving American youth what is justly his – guidance, training, discipline, proper surroundings, incentive, moral and spiritual development – is more important than ever before in the history of our Nation. The strength, the security, and the future of America depend upon the character and the quality of our youth."

Boys on a fishing trip.

Chapter 11: Law of Gravity

Reputation has a way of preceding some people. Seems ours had done just that. One Saturday evening, as we were walking up to our friend Ernie's house, a simple wooden house with rickety steps leading up onto a small porch, a police officer and Ernie's mother greeted us from the porch. Ernie was one of our early childhood friends who lived close to our dad, and we always looked forward to seeing him and the other kids around there when we were home on vacation. This summer vacation had already started off with adventure, and given the nature of the event that had precipitated a visit from the police, we knew that we would have to tough this one out.

Off to the police station we went. But after a half hour of questioning, and a foolproof alibi, we were let go. What was our alibi you might ask? Well, we were over on the other side of town spying on the police captain at Ruth's Place. We knew the captain went there on Saturday nights, and this would be no exception. Ruth was a purveyor of … Well, let's just say she wasn't selling pies, and none of the officers who arrested us were going to question the captain …

Children's Home girls and boys grew up as Methodists, although several of us have migrated to other churches with similar or closely related beliefs over the years. I personally find that many churches today are simply big businesses using religion as the message they "sell" with a lack of the true spirit. Some very good churches seek to save and nourish the soul, and those are worth finding and attending. The Children's Home taught the true meaning of religion and that was along the lines of the Ten Commandments. Nevertheless, they still had a tough time reigning in mischievousness. This story involves the part about mischievousness.

On occasion, we found certain churches with a high level of jumping around and rolling on the floor to be on the outside fringe of our way of worship. They were usually good people; they just seemed to us to have a unique way of worshiping. This particular high-action church met every Saturday evening around 6 o'clock. They would be in full swing around 6:30 or 7, with loud shouting, singing, and rolling around on the floor of the church. This type of behavior made my friends and me curious. I don't recall snakes in the crowd like some churches further up in the mountains, but I believe we saw one or two of the congregation levitating off the floor.

One night, Jimmy Bustle, Ernie Beach, Clifton Benge, Gilmer, and I were out looking for adventure. The Russians had recently launched Sputnik, and we had been practicing rocketry for quite some time. We were able to blast a rocket several hundred feet into the air using common chemicals that lads our age could roust up in no time. It usually culminated in the rocket exploding in the air. Needless to say, the chutes aboard never did deploy. They just added to the massive heavenly fire that ensued, sending everyone in our group, plus many unsuspecting townspeople, running for shelter, followed shortly by rumors of UFOs.

Along our way to adventure, we happened upon this Holy Roller church in session. We stopped to listen for a short while, amazed by the hollering and screaming. Ernie took the time to light up a Camel, and we just sat listening. It was then that this jewel of an idea to deploy our rockets burst onto the scene. Not sure where it came from. It seems as if it were planted in each of us simultaneously, though I think Gilmer actually uttered the words first.

Chapter 11: Law of Gravity

Here was a Holy Roller church in full swing; there in the back was a two-hole outhouse, one for men and one for women. As noted, someone (Gilmer) said something about the outhouse and a rocket. Off we went in different directions to get the makings of a rocket. Fifteen minutes later we had all returned, completely out of breath. We checked among each other and confirmed that we had all the necessary ingredients.

Our first impulse was to fire a rocket at the outhouse, but then we remembered that our past endeavors were not overly successful in aim or reliability. On an earlier occasion, we had attempted to launch a rocket from the top of the local water tower in pursuit of a height record, but only succeeding in blowing a large hole in the top. (This is the first time that has been made public, but I guess after fifty-five years the statute of limitations has expired.) Instead, we decided to throw a rocket into the outhouse and blow it over. More specifically, when Jimmy Bustle suggested that we throw two rockets into the outhouse, one with a long fuse into the hole and one with a short fuse in the outhouse itself, that suggestion immediately became our plan.

Quickly, we fashioned the "bombs" and inserted the fuses. The fuses were designed for underwater, as we used them to dynamite fish in the river – that was cheaper than buying fishing equipment and far more effective and faster. Soon, the fuses were lit, and the bombs were delivered in a flash. We all ran!

Inside the church, the piano was playing, people were singing in loud voices, and the preacher was shouting in tongues. But the evening had become uncannily quiet outside the church, too quiet. In fact, the quiet was deafening. Then the first homemade bomb exploded. It happened so suddenly and with such force that it made the ground shake. There was a large plume of smoke, and the outhouse doors were seen leaving the area. Then the outhouse slammed over onto its side. The roof was gone, but none of us saw where it landed. (It was later found on the roof of the church, having departed unnoticed through the plume of smoke.) We all were at the stage of sheer panic. We had grossly overloaded the charge … and a second was set to go. Given the results of the first, we could only imagine what the next would do.

At this point, everyone in the church and everything within two miles was quiet. No birds, no piano, no singing, no cars, no nothing. Then everything went flat-out bozo crazy. Men and women were pouring out of the back door of the church to see what had exploded. The smoke had somewhat cleared, and the brave men pushed through to get over near the outhouse. The preacher worked his way through the ladies and up to where the men were. He had no sooner said, "We'll get the bastards who did this" than the most unusual thing happened.

A sound was coming from beneath the ground where the outhouse had stood – somewhat like a ThaWhomp!!!!!!! Though it was a muffled sound, it handily shook the ground. It wasn't just the sickening sound or the ground shaking that got everyone's attention. It was this large and high plume of what had been beneath the two-holer for the past three years. Everyone was looking up in a frozen state of horror. Before any of the men had a chance to run back through the women, following the preacher, the law of gravity took effect and the rain of earthbound stink was fast upon them.

It was literally everyone for themselves. The men were shoving past the women close behind the preacher. You would have thought someone had shouted, "supper's ready!"

Oh, the sight that day! I will never forget it as long as I live. What was white or blue or red was now covered in large splatters of brown. There were no hats to save them, no trees to run under, no umbrellas, and no one holding their coats over the ladies except for one young man holding his coat over his girlfriend. There was only the cloud of slow motion liquid fertilizer descending at the speed of stink in a windstorm. It spared no one. Clothes were coming off everywhere. People were heading for their cars, but even their dogs were refusing to ride with them.

There was gagging and puking, and that was coming from Ernie, Jimmy, and Clifton. Gilmer and I were dying from laughter. We quickly disposed of what evidence was left and snuck back through the surrounding woods toward Ernie's house, where later we had a discussion with his mother and the police. This was a story we kept to ourselves.

Vacation was soon over, and we headed back to all our friends and to canning green beans, corn, and tomatoes.

*Sledding on Richard J. Reynolds hill with
sleds (top) and cardboard (bottom).*

Chapter 12:

The Train

"We frequently remind our staff of workers that the greatest factor in serving children who come to us is not our beautiful campus, our accommodating buildings or our motivating activities so much as the persons who direct the children in our buildings, who serve as good leaders on our campus and who direct our children's expressional activities with constructive resourcefulness. In our opinion, child care institutions will continue to be needed so long as they can constructively meet the increasing demands made upon them. If this is true, and we think it is, there must be much care used in the selection of leadership personnel and the way this personnel understandingly directs children."

Blackberry Rain

On the south side of the Children's Home campus was the Norfolk and Western railroad tracks. Passenger and freight trains would pass through about six or seven times a day, usually at a high rate of speed. Only occasionally would they sound their horn and that was deliberately to warn someone to be alert.

Richard J. Reynolds High School (RJR) was a little way west, across the road from our campus. It sat on top of a hill overlooking a large open field that sloped down to a wild rose briar-laden hedgerow. Once past this hedgerow, you were on to the Norfolk and Western railroad tracks, which paralleled the hedgerow.

A number of stories related to the railroad tracks circulated around the Home. These include the day somebody driving along Renolda Road reported two boys had been run over by a train, four boys were seen being knocked from the bridge over Peters Creek by a train, and the infamous slide down the hill at RJR. This is the story about the infamous slide down the hill at RJR.

When it snowed in North Carolina, on occasion the snow was so deep that everything shut down. School was canceled, people stayed home from work, and at the Children's Home kids got to enjoy the snow once their chores were done. This particular snow day was especially grand … six inches! Usually, one inch was enough for a mayoral decree. However, a six-inch snow in the middle of February when fun had all but come to a standstill … Wow! That is fantastic.

Once we knew that school had been canceled, we headed for the hill at RJR. This was a sledder's dream, and we had the fastest sled going, a four-foot by five-foot piece of heavy cardboard. In those days, we didn't have plastic or aluminum snow pans and couldn't afford wooden toboggans or railed sleds. But hey, who cared, we could get down the hill faster than anyone else because we waxed the bottom of the cardboard, using paste wax from the Norfleet cottage floor supply. Boy, it was slick!

Most of the kids on the hill were from Buena Vista, a well-to-do area of homes just north of RJR and west of the Home. With the exception of a few, those kids weren't like us. They tended to play it safe most of the time, whereas we were always looking for challenges and were ready to face them head-on.

There were two ways to get to RJR from our campus. One was a shortcut over a large steel pipe and up through the woods. This steel pipe traversed a creek that was about twenty feet wide and about two feet deep at that point. However, the pipe itself was suspended six feet above the creek – one misstep, and you were soaked. But it wasn't the getting soaked that concerned us. It was being labeled for eternity as not being able to "walk the pipe." And it was not only the Home boys who walked the pipe; many Home girls did, too.

The second way to get to RJR was a bit longer. It was down the length of the campus and across a footbridge and up a long winding path to the top of the hill. Well, unbeknownst to most, there was also a third way. We called it the "Calmadge way," named after Calmadge Jones, a Home boy, who used to sneak out the back gate and walk through Buena Vista to RJR because he didn't want people to know he was from the Home. Calmadge would always bury his face in his hands when Principal Jordan would announce that all Children's Home boys were dismissed to get in hay or harvest potatoes. The rest of us Home boys would laugh because we asked Tandy, the assistant principal, to have the announcement made, and he did so time and time again, as we were harvesting hay throughout the late spring and early summer, and potatoes in early fall. Tandy was pretty kind to us Home boys. He helped us through some difficult studies through his tutoring.

But most of us were proud to be Home kids because we had fun and had great sports teams. Besides, we had the prettiest girls around – all the RJR boys were firing on them.

Okay, so here we were, six inches of snow and hundreds of kids. Where to sled? The most pristine part of the RJR hill was a run that went down the hill, under the bushes, and right down to the railroad track. Two summers before, some of us had cut a hole in the bushes large enough to allow us to get through to the tracks. It made a great sled run, but what if a train would come? For fear of the train, everyone steered away from that run; everyone. Nevertheless, after giving it some thought, I decided I would try it, but wanted to scout it out first.

Then there she was, my true love, Anna Brown. (Her real name is secret. I only use the real names of the Home boys and girls because you can do that with family.) This was the girl who had started panic in several classrooms by screaming RAAAATTTTT!!!! during a highly attended, much-anticipated movie about the Industrial Revolution. That incident was the subject of a previous story entitled "Flying Squirrels."

Anna was walking directly toward me but ignored me just enough to cause me to blurt out, "Hey, wanna go down the hill?" To my astonishment she said yes. To this day I don't know why, but I said, "Why don't we try this fresh snow?" She agreed, since there was no one on this part of the slope. In my excitement, it didn't occur to me that nobody was there because it led to a narrow walkway crossing an iron-railed footbridge over a creek!!!

By then it was too late to change the run. We sat down on the cardboard – Anna in front and I in back. Somehow, it seemed the brave thing for me to do. With that we pushed off.

Circumstance has a way of developing into something good or something you simply put out of your mind for over fifty years. As circumstance would have it in this case, as we gained speed, the white powder blasted from the front of the cardboard right into Anna's face. It was instant freeze. The freeze lasted only till about halfway down this quarter mile of zigging and zagging toward the creek. Suddenly we started screaming as we saw the bridge walk fast approaching. I think I started screaming first but would never admit to it, as was our way.

Word has it that the first two people on the bridge we encountered coming toward us flipped over us and landed on the cardboard sled, which had come to a sudden stop when we hit the bridge. With our speed, we simply continued without it, plowing into several other kids, who ended up pushing snow into a pile ahead of them. All in all, there were seven people in the heap. No one was hurt, and everyone started laughing. In fact, they were talking to Anna as if she was a brave and magnificent sledder. I used this distraction to escape back to the top of the hill, taking what was left of our sled with me.

Arriving at the top of the hill, I surveyed the damage to the magnificent sled and found it to be about eight inches narrower as a result of the collision with the bridge. Other than that, it was still in order. Within minutes, Anna appeared by my side, saying how much she had enjoyed our ride, even though she had been a little frightened. However, she added that I sure knew how to sled and that had made her feel better. Little did she know that was the first time I ever made that run. I had done it a few times on a flexi, a four-wheeled, low-to-the-ground ride-of-your-life-guided sled of sorts, but never on snow!

At the top of the hill and on the steps leading up to the RJR auditorium, quite a crowd of kids was gathering, and everyone was trying to see who could go the longest distance. Emboldened by the last run down the hill, Anna wanted to give it a try, too. With her newfound courage, she issued a challenge, grabbed our sled, and headed for the front of the crowd. Everyone started cheering. We jumped on the cardboard wonder and got a hard push from someone in the crowd. A Home kid no doubt, as it was a very strong push.

There is something about trains that can send fear into the hearts of even the bravest. Sometimes you just can't be far enough away from them. They are big and powerful, and can sneak up on you with uncanny silence. I totally understand why cows and horses run when trains cross through the countryside.

As Anna and I pushed off, I steered our sled down the hill toward the opening in the briar hedge. Going that far would set the record and leave it impossible to beat. Anna was laughing and yelling as we lunged forward, her bravery in all its glory. But as we got farther down the hill, her laughter and the crowd's cheering started to turn to silence. And then, when we got close to the wild rose hedge and continued to gain speed on the waxed wonder, the silence turned to a scream that sounded much like stoooooooooooop!!!!!! The crowd was screaming because they saw what we couldn't see – a train, Apparently, the train's engineer also saw us. As Anna and I continued sliding at what seemed to be right around the speed of sound, and just as we got to the opening in the bushes, the train's whistle blew.

I swear to this day that Anna's hair stood straight on end as absolute terror grabbed her! I think she saw her life flash before her that day between the beginning of the opening in the bushes and the flight through the air on the other side. In mid-air, after passing through the bushes, all I could see through her standing-straight-hair was an enormous, fast, loud freight train, every bit as big as a barn.

Several brave high school girls slid down through the opening, screaming for us. At first they didn't see us. I was completely buried, and all they could see was Anna's motionless head sticking out of the snow, her eyes closed. I'm sure they thought she was dead from being hit by the train. As I came up from beneath the snow bank, I was gasping for air. The girls started to scream. That brought Anna to, and she started to scream, too. Soon everybody was screaming! The boys on the other side of the bushes thought the train had killed us and also started screaming and crying.

At that moment, I started laughing. It just happened; I couldn't help it. I didn't realize what all the commotion was, but I knew that we were okay and that this was yet another hilarious moment of scaring the unsuspecting. Boy, my sick sense of humor. Earlier in the day, I had wanted to scout out the opening in the bushes to find out what was on the other side. Well, I did!

Just past the opening was a big drop-off with a large snow bank a good thirty feet from the tracks and ten feet below them. There was no way for us to reach the tracks. We were buried in the snow bank. I just hadn't counted on the train coming by at that time. That was perfect timing!

By the time we reached the top of the hill, everything was fine again. The girls were laughing, and the Buena Vista boys were trying hard to hide the fact that they had been screaming and crying. Anna left to go and change her clothes. I too left to get a change of clothes. She not only wet herself, she also wet me … at least that's my story, and I'm sticking to it! Something about an unexpected train and a loud, very loud, train whistle while we were in mid-air.

CHAPTER 13:

Blackberry Rain

"We have been tremendously busy here of late. As a matter of fact, we think we are never otherwise. There is always something to do. Our policy is to do the next thing and let the one following it, and those others we know will then come along, take their turn. It is the next thing with us, unless some abrupt annoyance comes along. Too frequently such happens."

Boys picking beans.

Chapter 13: Blackberry Rain

I've given up on trying to protect the innocent, as most of the boys and girls we hung with were anything but innocent, but still didn't do anything outrageously bad. Usually the girls, who were in charge of doing the campus laundry, would starch our shirts so stiff that we could break the sleeve trying to put the shirt on. The collar would rub our necks raw. Not to be undone, some of the boys would punish other boys by leaving a pair of their underwear on the girls' side of the campus in the middle of the road, with their name showing – usually carried on a stick as no one would touch dirty underwear with their bare hands.

Somewhere between the age of twelve and sixteen, boys on at the Children's Home would learn to drive. This might be through instructions from one of the driving adults, or in most cases by "borrowing" the tractor or dairy truck. Sometimes we had to learn out of necessity in order to get in hay, pick up a load of newly harvested sweet potatoes, deliver coal to the cottages, or take the morning's fresh-picked produce to the staff and kitchens.

To this day, I don't remember a chore that wasn't turned into fun, except grinding and mixing feed. That was an incredibly dusty job. Sam Vickory was the only guy I knew who enjoyed "sacking feed." That person held the sacks under the chute from which the ground and mixed feed flowed. He would come out of the mill covered in white dust, looking like a ghost! To scare the girls, he would drag his leg, make a strange gurgling sound, and walk straight toward them. Without fail, this would scare the bejeezus out of them.

Getting back to driving. It was in the summer of 1957 and I had been blackberry picking. Most of the kids had gone to Buena Vista, a neighboring, well-to-do area of town, to look for Saturday jobs to make extra money. We would go from house to house asking if they had any chores for us to do. It usually entailed washing windows, mowing lawns, or working in their gardens. The pay was good (fifty cents to one dollar an hour) and made up nicely for the honorarium Gilmer and I rarely got. Children's Home boys and girls received an honorarium based upon their performance for the past month. Unfortunately for Gilmer and me, our conduct was usually so bad that we rarely saw rewards. Fact was, had they known about the fun we had getting into trouble, we would have owed them money. We thought getting into trouble was a sport!

Okay, on this particular Saturday, I had picked a gallon of the nicest blackberries ever. They were large, firm, and very sweet. We had had the perfect rain, called a blackberry rain, in May when the blackberries were in bloom. It paid off very nicely, as a kind old lady in Buena Vista gave me four dollars for the gallon and let me keep the bucket. That, ladies and gentlemen, boys and girls, and children of all ages, was a home run!! An hour and a half of work, and I was rich!! Highly motivated and rewarded, off I went to pick another gallon.

The blackberry patch was located between the creek and the orchard that belonged to the Home. I ran back as fast as I could without drawing attention. At the Children's Home, the sight of a boy running meant that he was up to no good, and rumor carried across the wind to Tula Harrison, the Goddess of Threatened Punishment, within moments. Paul Booze and B. L. Angel, the truck farm and big farm managers, would be dispatched with haste, and any fun would be brought to a screeching halt. Having dodged rumors on the wind, I started picking.

I had picked several mouthfuls, as required for children of all ages, and was leaning in toward the center of the patch, within reach of the mother lode. Like all Children's Home boys, I had an uncanny ability to sense when something wasn't just right. The hair stood up on the back of my head and my mouth got dry. Out of the corner of my eye, I saw something move ever so slowly. As I turned my head at the speed of one inch an hour, I saw a blacksnake the size of Texas within arm's reach.

My first impulse, prompted by sheer fear, was to yell and jump straight up into thin air and cling to a cloud, to lunge straight ahead through the tangle of briars, pulling them out and dragging them with me as I ran hell bent for leather. But then my Children's Home boy mischievousness kicked in. No one had ever caught a blacksnake this big … no one. This by itself would be good for two, maybe three, months of "hero" status, the ultimate in bragging rights!!

Ever so slowly I lowered my blackberries. I looked at the blacksnake's position and realized he was up in the bush close to me, coiled around several blackberry branches with a good part of him still on the ground. Was he ever huge! The snake wasn't in a very good running (slithering) position, but then neither was I. At that moment, I did what surprised even me. Instinctively, in a flash, my hand shot out and grabbed the snake just behind the head and held tight, very tight. The blacksnake instantly coiled around my arm, covering it all the way up to my shoulder. His mouth gaped open, as he started to hiss. I pulled back from the bushes and literally flew to the dairy barn, a half-mile down the pasture, one eye on the snake's head and the other on the blackberry bushes through which I was weaving in and out. To this day, I don't recall my feet ever touching the ground. I didn't see the creek I crossed. I didn't feel the wind. It was all one big blur.

At the barn, I found an empty feed sack and proceeded to unwrap the snake off my arm and slide it into the sack.

Getting a closer look, I estimated the blacksnake to be over six feet long and as big around in the middle as my upper arm. I tied the sack tight, very, very tight.

Having accomplished this feat, I ran around the dairy looking for someone to brag to. No one was in sight. As I came around the milk room, I ran smack dab into Roy Benge. After catching my breath for the first time since I saw the snake, I somewhat calmly told him of capturing the blacksnake. He wanted proof and demanded to see it. I showed him the sack, and he could see that it was moving. Being deadly afraid of snakes, he went on to say he didn't actually need to see it.

Then Roy had an idea. He wanted to put this black wonder in the mailbox of a boy who lived over on Renolda Road, in a well-to-do neighborhood near the Home. I'm not sure why he wanted to do this and didn't ask. I think he just wanted to pull a "harmless" prank on the guy. We had to wait to carry out the deed until later that night when we could get the truck without anyone noticing. We decided that Roy would wake me up with the 3 a.m. milk crew and we would then deliver the present.

Just as agreed, Roy woke me at three o'clock, and together we went down to the barn. I grabbed the snake from my hiding place and he told me to follow him. Then we went around to the dairy pickup truck, and proceeded to push it past the barn and down the back road toward the pasture leading to the orchard. No one saw … or heard … us.

After what seemed like an eternity, we jumped into the truck and Roy started it. We drove up through the pasture and out the back gate near the little white church. Now at a safe distance from the Home, he turned on the headlights and we headed toward Renolda Road. I had somewhat dozed off when all of a sudden I noticed that we were going from one side of the road to the other. Wide-awake, I looked over at

Chapter 13: Blackberry Rain

Roy and saw him slumped over the steering wheel. I struggled to steer the truck and we careened off the road into a yard. The truck stopped. In my desperation to wake Roy, I completely forgot about the snake.

Roy finally came to, and immediately jumped out of and away from the truck, gasping. I thought he was having a fit. He grabbed me and heavily breathed the only word he could get out, "Run!!" "Run!!" was kind of the Children's Home boys' motto, most of the time uttered by Gilmer or me when trying to escape or somehow get out of a scrape.

Roy and I ran back a mile or so to the orchard and headed for the dairy. Roy told me, "Don't tell anyone about this." I never did till now, not even to my brothers.

Later I learned from Roy that he was driving barefoot. While I had been dozing, the snake had escaped through a hole in the sack and was lying across my lap, across the center seat, sprawled down onto the floor and across onto Roy's bare foot. When Roy looked over, he saw nothing but snake, felt the cold snake across his foot and starting up his leg, and all the blood rushed from his head … quite simply, he fainted!! The truck ended up on the lawn of a very large home on Renolda Road. No damage was done to the lawn or the truck.

Neither Roy nor I ever discussed that ride. We could never tell anyone about the largest blacksnake ever captured. The truck in the yard remained a mystery, but word was that the house went up for sale a few days later … something about the lady of the house and a very large blacksnake …

I'm sure Tula Harrison heard from the wind who had done it, but she never let on that she knew.

Boys running race.

Girls cheering for their team.

CHAPTER 14:

Injustice

"The Children's Home family is in the play business as a means to an end. When we come to estimate the value of play in terms of character, as such is measured by actions, we are overwhelmingly convinced that playing pays. It is certainly a most worthwhile character producing agency. Fine attitudes are crystallized, wholesome activities are promoted and encouraging results are recorded. Interesting play will tend to transform sullen, grouchy, self-centered youngsters, sitting around on their lower ends, into up and going enthusiastic young people who use their upper ends. By this time it is doubtless evident to our readers that we here at the Children's Home believe in play."

Blackberry Rain

It was a hot summer Saturday at the Home. It was almost always hot in the summertime, especially if you were hoeing corn or practicing for the upcoming football season.

There was a feeling of excitement in the air as we drew nearer the football field. We were going to play a game of flag football. It was not just an ordinary game; this time the girls would be playing with the boys. That meant only one thing: The chance to prove once and for all that Judy Dusenbary was not faster than all the boys. This was a matter of pride. In fact, we thought there was a law against girls being better than boys at anything, except, of course, ironing and laundry. A comment like that heard by any of the girls would mean the certain "you'll never get your hands through that starched Sunday shirt." The girls ruled the laundry, and any boy who was in a beef with them could wind up in a starched shirt that would almost break if you dropped it. They could starch a shirt so hard it would rub the back of your neck raw before Sunday school was over.

Teams were chosen, with a certain slant toward those who were out to prove that boys were superior being selected for the team opposing Judy Dusenbary. Battle had hardly begun when they gave her the ball. It was time to prove our superiority. Off she darted toward the left side of the field. All the boys on the defensive team were fast after her. Winfred Hammer and Walter Jones were within a step of catching her, when she suddenly turned and darted back behind them. Our two best were grabbing air. Graham and I (Gilmer) were the next closest to her and ran smack dab into each other as she hurtled between us. Whoosh ... she scored. What humiliation! Wilbur Brown and Lynwood Saterfield had slowed a bit as they thought we had her.

Chapter 14: Injustice

Given this letdown, it was time for tactics. We would form a circle the next time Judy received the ball; there would be no escape. After about twenty minutes of play and a few good tricks of our own, the score was evened to one touchdown each. It was their ball. Here it came, the handoff to Judy Dusenbary, the freckled wonder. Our plan was immediately put into action. Judy was zigging and zagging so fast that we were barely able to stay up with her. Just as Grady Lord was reaching for the flag, she zigged instead of zagged, and slipped down as the circle was closing. Down went Judy Dusenbary, and Grady Lord. A pile-up ensued with me on top of Judy and Grady, followed by Graham, Wilbur Brown, Winfred Hammer, Mike Ashton, Lynwood, and Hilda Smyth. Hilda later said she was pulling the boys off.

From the bottom of the pile, I saw my chance to inflict a bit of justice. There across Grady Lord's back, and right in front of my mouth, was Judy Dusenbary's arm. It said very loudly, "Bite Me." So I did!

The scream was not only deafening to those on the pile; it was so loud and piercing that it was also heard by Home Mothers Miss Reynolds, Tula Harrison, the Goddess of Threatened Punishment, who was sneaking a smoke, and by Miss Little, who happened to be walking the campus taking in the beauty of the day. They all ran onto the field and into the fray. Tula was hurling boys off the heap when she came upon Judy Dusenbary. Judy was playing the pain to the hilt, screaming and crying as if a mad dog had bitten her. When asked what was wrong, how was she hurt, she displayed her arm with the double teeth marks. It was as though a cloud of cold rain had swept over everyone. Tula Harrison peered around to see who had the guilt of Cain on their face. No one moved a muscle or showed any sign of emotion outwardly ... inside we all wanted to run.

Since Judy Dusenbary could not identify who had bitten her, Miss Harrison resorted to the famous "line-up." This was the customary thing to do when investigating a dastardly deed by one of the boys. Since it was somewhat routine, we knew to fall in line. Then came the cunning investigative techniques only Tula Harrison could deploy: matching teeth with the bite marks. I saw a sound whopping coming, or worse, Tula's "I'll put you in a sack and mop the floor with you" threat. Every boy feared this threat, though I can't say that I had ever witnessed it carried out. It was legend, and no one doubted it or wanted to experience it first-hand.

There was a second Christmas for me that year. Graham had gotten in line just ahead of me, or should I say, I had gotten in line behind Graham. Being twins did have its good points. The matching of teeth was quite simple. Miss Harrison made each boy put his teeth over the bite marks on Judy Dusenbary's arm so she, Miss Little, and Miss Reynolds could verify a possible match. This is where being twins came in. Graham's teeth were an exact match with mine. I didn't want my brother to get in trouble, but ...

One by one the boys had to put their teeth over the bite marks. Wilbur Brown, no. Grady Lord, no. Mike Ashton, no. Bill Dobbers, no. Lynwood Saterfield, no. Walter Jones, no. Winfred Hammer, yes ...YES ...Winfred Hammer, yes?!! What happened, how could it happen? Winfred Hammer's teeth were a perfect match? No question. Justice was swift and immediate. The last time we saw or heard Winfred that day was when Tula Harrison had him by one ear with his feet barely touching the ground, on his way to parts and punishment unknown, all the while denying, denying, denying!

Chapter 14: Injustice

We had just missed a certain and sure punishment worse than the infamous "ditch" or Coach Clary's paddle. We had been spared a fate worse than having a pair of our underwear showing up on the girls' side of campus.

To this day we have never told anyone this story, and certainly not Winfred. If anyone tells Winfred, we'll deny, deny, deny!

George Poole and Gilmer and Graham Murdock.

CHAPTER 15:

Mongoose

"There are those who celebrate over the number of social workers they have in their organization and the great volume of service such workers are able to do. All glory to them and may their tribe increase. So far as the Children's Home is concerned we simply admit that we have no social worker with the rating usually called for. We are content with doing the job at hand without much celebration and without much ado about it. We only rise up and speak out when the intimation is made that our work is either poorly done or limitedly done. We feel assured that what other organizations may do or not do is in line with their own wish and ability. We also feel assured that our challenge is being assumed in line with our own wish and ability."

One of the great moments at the Children's Home was the annual announcement of summer vacations. Don't get me wrong. It was hard to leave our extended family of brothers and sisters, but it is hard to beat three weeks where we would get to eat just about any junk food we wanted and sleep in whenever we wanted.

Our brother Jim and his wife, Melda, who were living in Baltimore, Maryland, invited us to stay with them for several of these vacations. That was an especially glorious treat as we were able to travel to another part of the world. One of the spectacular parts of the journey was crossing the Chesapeake Bay Bridge. That was enough to keep your heart in your throat as we went up and over.

Jim loved to play practical jokes on people and had been involved in the "silk purse" incident. On one of our vacation visits to Jim and Melda, Jim invited us to help build a mongoose box. It was about two feet long, one foot wide, and six inches high. There was a wire mesh cage in the front with an entry hole for the mongoose to go into the back wood-enclosed portion and hide-away. On the top, there was an opening through which you could put things into or remove things from the cage.

In 1959 Gilmer and I joined the Marines. On occasion, we found ourselves back at Jim and Melda's home. On one such trip we brought three women Marines with us. They wanted to get away from Quantico, Virginia, where they were stationed, for a long weekend, but traveling to Illinois, where they were from, was a bit far, so we invited them along to Baltimore. The girls were Rhonda Reye, Billy Jo, and Sue Ellen. Each of these girls was prompt for all three Marine Corps meals each day. They were not girls with whom you wanted to pick a fight. They could all bench press over 200 pounds.

Chapter 15: Mongoose

On this particular trip, we decided to go to a baseball game. I'm not sure who the Orioles were playing or what the final score was as we spent most of our time in the beer and chow lines. And even at that, we were all still hungry when we headed home.

When we got home, Jim wanted to show the girls where they were going to sleep, in the downstairs bedrooms. We, along with the three girls, walked down the stairs and were heading toward one of the bedrooms when Rhonda Reye noticed the mongoose box sitting on a piece of newspaper on a large oak table. She started toward it, asking Jim what it was. He immediately stepped in front of her and said, "Hon, you had best be very careful with that, as it is the home of our pet mongoose. He can be very mean if you awaken him suddenly. In fact, he has severely bitten people who aggravated him."

With that all three girls became curious and asked if they could see the mongoose. Jim said yes, but warned them that they must stand back a few feet. Stepping behind the table, Jim told Rhonda Reye that if she leaned forward a bit and tapped on the cage, she might be able to awaken the mongoose. Excited, Rhonda Reye and the other girls got a bit closer and could see the large fluffy tail sticking out of the hole. Their curiosity was piqued. Unbeknownst to them, Jim had picked up a small file, and as Rhonda Reye tapped on the cage, he ran the file along the back of the cage, making it sound like a growl. The girls moved back a little upon hearing the sound, but Jim assured them that the mongoose was just a bit grumpy and if Rhonda Reye tapped again, it should awaken him.

Again the three girls, women Marines all, moved closer, and Rhonda Reye again tapped on the cage, this time a bit harder. Jim moved the file over the back and made an even louder sound. Then he said, "Tap harder," to which Rhonda Reye responded with a hard rap!

In the flash of a millisecond, something with a large bushy tail flew out of the top of the cage and hit Rhonda Reye square in the chest. With her eyes bulging out, she gasped several times, and all she could do was run in place, flailing her arms and screaming at the top of her voice, "IT'S LOOSE, IT'S LOOSE, THE MONGOOSE IS LOOSE!!!!!!!!"

Billy Jo and Sue Ellen bolted for the stairwell and got there at precisely the same instant, screaming and trying to get up the stairs. Bouncing along erratically on the floor was this mad monster animal with its large, fluffy tail. As far as the girls knew, it was looking for someone to bite!! Neither Billy Jo nor Sue Ellen could budge, as they were wedged tight in the stairwell. All three girls peed in their pants!!

When the screaming and crying stopped and the sheer terror left to stories untold, the girls started to look around. There on the floor at Rhonda Reye's feet was a large, fluffy tail tied to a rubber ball. Her last, rather commanding tap on the cage had triggered Jim to pull the spring-loaded trap door that caused a loud mechanical squeal and hurled the ball and tail right into Rhonda Reye's chest.

That is the closest I have ever come to seeing a house being carried away. The banister was crushed into the wall at the bottom of the stairs.

It was about an hour before any of the girls would talk. There was great silence for the remainder of the night and on our drive back to the base the next day. Halfway there,

Chapter 15: Mongoose

a squirrel ran across the road, and we did everything we could to hold the car on the road, because of the screaming and bouncing of the girls in the back seat. Gilmer and I were never so glad to wave goodbye to somebody as after this trip … even though nobody returned our waves!!

Aurelia Bowman Building, Central Dining Hall.

Give Us This Day Our Daily Bread

"There must be a morale connected with the living conditions of any company of people, particularly growing people, children and youths in their immaturity. Their habit formations and their outlook on life are of serious moment and consequence. With this in mind we are continually rethinking conditions that have to do with the proper upbringing of our children. We frankly admit that the last word had not been said in regard to this challenge."

The year was approximately 1956. One day every month or so was cause for great anticipation by all the boys at the Children's Home. It's not Christmas, though if you were one of the Home kids you might think it was. Every so often, Merrita Bread Company in Winston Salem would bring out a large load of stale bread and cakes to our pigpen. The goodies were unloaded in a shed and later fed to the pigs, paper and all. In those days, the bread and cakes were wrapped in paper, and the pigs knew no difference between the paper or the bread and cake, and from the way they ate them, they didn't care.

We raised about 100 hogs and slaughtered them in late fall of each year, depending on age and size. Each of us participated in this event, which included shooting the hog, bleeding it, dumping it into a vat of scalding water, and scraping all the hair off it. It was then hung up on a tripod and cut up into various sections for either the smokehouse or the freezers. We used most everything off the hog, and what we didn't use we sold to someone who could find a use for it. Nothing went to waste. The boys and girls alike loved the crackling cakes, made from the skin from the hogs, cut into pieces and deep-fried. We made the best!

Merrita bread day was like no other day of the year. In fact, it was a day of unparalleled communication between the boys and girls on the campus. Within fifteen minutes of a Merrita bread truck or one of our own trucks loaded with Merrita bread hitting the campus gate, the word had spread to every boy and girl of age and interest. The moment this happened, plans were immediately set into action. It was an unwritten rule that no one referred to the bread delivery as anything but "bread." No one ever mentioned "cake." We acted oblivious to this fact, though we knew, and they knew we knew.

Chapter 16: Give Us This Day Our Daily Bread

The pigpen was on the upper end of the campus in a north-eastwardly direction. It was far enough from the main campus so we did not hear, see, or smell the pigs. The wind rarely, if ever, blew from that direction. If you didn't know it was there, you wouldn't guess, unless you lived in Chatham, a poor neighborhood, close to campus.

There was only one time during the year when you could smell anything from that end of the campus, and that came from the dairy. Each spring, we would clean the manure out of the barns and spread it on the pastures. In previous years we used a mule-drawn wagon, then a mule-drawn manure spreader, and finally a tractor-drawn manure spreader. Either way, Home boys loaded them all with pitchforks and strong backs.

Plans for the Merrita bread day called for every boy and girl to play a role. There were the distracters, those who made a subtle but effective action to distract the Home Mothers by meeting with them over some inconsequential matter. There were the lookouts, who made certain to warn everyone in the event someone of authority was heading for the pigpen. Only boys who could whistle loudly were chosen as lookouts. Then there were the actual retrievers, the privileged few who would get the cakes from the locked and secure pigpen feed room, the bravest of the brave.

The girls' involvement in this great effort consisted of distracting the senior help. This was usually in the form of a laundry machine malfunction, a window stuck in one of the dorm rooms, or a broken clothesline, one by one, causing the staff to be distracted from the upper end of the campus.

The large shed at the pigpen contained unshucked corn, sacks of mixed grain, and a storage area for the occasional

Merrita bread delivery. This area was always locked. The only ways into the bread section of the shed were through the door if you had a key, which was guarded about as well as the key to the peaches in the cannery, or through a window. The window was one and a half stories up from where the pigs were slopped. This area was, let's just say, a "muddy" mess. The only way to the window was up a tree, a six-foot jump to the roof, and a walk along the narrow edge of the roof. You then had to blindly reach around the corner of the roof and grab the side of the window. If you hadn't fallen by now, you could pull yourself very hard and swing onto the window ledge. Thank goodness this window was never locked as it provided much-needed air circulation for the shed, and our entry.

On this particular day, everything was falling into place. Jerry Murdock, John Tuttle, and Roy Benge were the retrievers. Lookouts were in place, and distracters were in action.

Jerry was the first brave soul to attempt the cross-over. The move from the tree to the side of the shed was almost a disaster. As he jumped and landed, the shingle he landed on broke loose and slipped. He desperately grabbed for the roof and teetered for a moment. There was solid roof or sure slop. Fortunately, he was able to get his balance and hold on to the roof. Nevertheless, this didn't make the others feel any more confident. In fact, it made them more nervous, knowing what was in store for them.

The next move was the blind swing over to the window. This was going to be tougher as Jerry's heart was already in his throat from the earlier near fall. But there was no choice but to continue, as a Home boy could never exhibit fear. Doing so would visit a plague upon him and his friends. So with eyes closed, Jerry swung hard around the corner of the roof to the window. He made it!!

Once inside, he began the frantic search for cakes and found the mother lode!! He shouted to Roy and John that it was full of cakes. John could hardly wait. He flew off the tree onto the roof, moved along the edge, and swung into the window as if he had done it a hundred times. Roy was next. He could hardly wait either, but as he jumped to the roof, disaster struck. The roof shingle that Jerry had slipped on now came completely off. Roy was off balance and desperately swung around toward the window, but it was too much of a reach. He fell backwards into the squealing pigs and all the foulness of slop and pig xsdz!?@. The fall knocked the wind out of him, and he ended up lying among the pigs, who were hoping to be fed. In the meantime, Jerry and John were busy stuffing their mouths and their shirts full of cakes. Each had deliberately worn a shirt a couple of sizes too big in order to maximize the load they could carry.

Roy finally caught his breath and somewhat regained his composure. His backside was covered with whatever it is pigs are covered with. There was no shame in falling, but there was shame in not completing the mission. He knew that tasty sweet cakes were awaiting him, and he could hardly wait. So back up the tree Roy went. He jumped on to the roof and made a solid landing. But just as he was swinging toward the window, they all heard the dreaded warning whistle at a distance. Then it was heard closer, and then it was heard only a couple of hundred yards away. This was the signal that someone was coming, and from the sound of it, whoever it was was coming fast. Absolute panic ensued.

The bravest of the brave sprang into action. The well-rehearsed plan of climbing carefully out the window, onto the roof, and down the tree, saving as many cakes as possible in the process, was completely forgotten. It was every man for himself. Again the great words of wisdom were uttered … "RUN, RUN!"

As Roy was reaching around for the window in a blind grab, Jerry and John were pushing out of the window, each trying to be first. They all met on the outer edge, and all three lost their balance and fell to the foulness below. This time Roy fell face forward as did John. Jerry landed on his feet but slipped down. What cakes they had had were no more. The impact of all three of them literally exploded cake and pig crap all over them. The pigs were squealing and running.

After recovering, they made a mad dash down the hill toward the creek. Out of the corner of their eyes, they saw the farm manager, B. L. Angel, in his pickup truck with a high plume of dust behind him. He was looking over toward the pigpen. They dove into the creek and crawled on their bellies for over half a mile. After that, it took them a couple of hours to wash the stench off themselves and their clothes.

Between the three of them, they ended up with only two cakes that were clean. They gave those to Roy, who shared with them on the spot. Only after a couple of hours did they feel safe to conclude that they hadn't been caught. Each went their separate way and showed up at the cottage at different times. Normal activities were going on all around them, and no one seemed to be the wiser.

Later that night, three other Home boys made the raid, this time with great success. They used sacks, and only one boy went into the shed while two others waited outside. The one in the shed was Gilmer. Walter Jones and I helped in the raid. The cakes were hidden in the hayloft of the lower barn. They could stay there for days prior to distribution, as we simply pinched off any mold and had fresh cake again. This treasure of cakes was distributed to all who participated in the raid that day as well as on the night trip.

At the Home, we always had a backup plan!

Some years ago at a Children's Home Homecoming, we were talking to B. L. Angel about the pigpen raids. He was quite gracious and suggested that they must have been a great source of fun for us kids. After pausing for a while, he said that they were also a great source of fun for him and the Home staff. They always knew when we were going to be there and had Merrita Bread deliver extra "good" cakes just so we would be rewarded for our ingenuity. He said that it was always a great source of gut-busting laughter at the Home staff meetings.

Boys bringing in the hay.

Fresh-Baked Bread

"A recapitulation indicates that on the first day of January, 1952, there were 415 boys and girls enrolled here with us, 210 boys and 205 girls. Our family continues to be large. Just about the time we get ready to reduce the number of children in a given building some very pressing reasons are offered for acceptance of other children who need care and direction. It may be true that our groups of youngsters in our various buildings are too large. In discussing with our staff members the desire not to overload them but to give them as many deserving youngsters as they can direct, we have observed through many years their readiness to accept the new children. A Home Mother can direct a larger number of youngsters when careful co-operation exists. Our slogan continues to be, 'The greatest good to the greatest number.'"

There were seasonal chores each month for the boys at the Children's Home. The girls had their share of responsibility but this is being told from one lad's perspective. Here are the chores listed by month:

January   Sorting potatoes, stored for winter consumption, and discarding bad ones

February   Preparing cold frames (used for growing seedlings early in the season to give plants a head start) made of wood frames with glass tops and filled with clean, enriched soil

March   Cleaning out the barns, planting seeds in cold frames

April   Planting tomatoes and potatoes from seedlings grown in cold frames, both according to the moon phase

May   Combining wheat and oats and getting in straw; picking strawberries and sneaking mouthfuls

June   Picking and canning peaches; picking and canning peas; stealing cherries from neighbor's tree

July   Picking/canning black-eyed peas, beans, tomatoes, and sweet corn; throwing tomatoes at friends

August   Bailing hay, mixing grain, swimming in ponds and river. Blindly running from water moccasins

September   Harvesting turnips and collard greens

October   Raking leaves campus-wide; delivering coal to all cottages from the coal car on the train siding

Chapter 17: Fresh-Baked Bread

November   Slaughtering hogs and making our famous
            "crackling cakes"

December   Spreading straw in the barns and practicing
            being really, really good for Christmas

All the above was in addition to the ongoing daily chores of
milking cows, cleaning cottages, helping in the kitchens, as
well as hoeing and picking crops and participating in school,
church, and sports. Everyone had assigned responsibilities
and everyone did them well.

The gist of this story is "cleaning out the barns." Every winter
in late November, all the milk cows and beef cows were moved
into their respective barns. They were permitted to wander in
a rather spacious yard, both at the lower and the upper barn.
But they were not permitted in the main pastures because it
would be too wet, and they would tear them up over winter,
and there was little or no forage … that is grass.

Throughout the summer, hay was harvested and put into
storage up in the lofts of three large barns; the lower barn
for milk cows, the milk barn for feeding the cows a special
diet before and after milking, and the upper barn for beef
cattle. We also had a calf barn, and some hay and grain was
stored there as well. Finally, grain was stored in the center
barn, or milk barn. This was grain we had mixed in our own
mill using predetermined formulas.

In the wintertime, every day after the 3:00 p.m. milking, some
of us were assigned to throw down bales of straw from the
loft and "bed down" the cattle. This helped keep them dry and
warm. In addition, we would feed each milk cow a certain diet
of hay and grain, according to their particular menu. This was
done to ensure good health and maximum milk production. All
the cows had a name and an assigned stanchion.

There was a standing rule in spreading bales of hay: to absolutely, positively, remove all the bailing twine. In the spring when cleaning out the barns, there was nothing worse than forking manure and getting about halfway through a manure load on a pitchfork throw and have a piece of twine catch in the manure. Twang ... it goes over everybody, and that is not a good thing!

Grady Lord, Sam Vickory, Ward McCullom, Gilmer, and I were assigned to help clean out the milk barn. I use the term "assigned" a bit loosely here. That usually meant you had been caught doing something wrong and this was the staff's way to help you to see and understand your wrongdoing. Ward usually was not part of the group being punished, but sometimes "association" is enough to force suspicion.

On this particular day, we were joined by three new kids. They were a couple of years younger than us and had never worked the dairy before. (As kids aged, their chores changed, and they moved up to replace those who had graduated and left the Home.) At any rate, they had somehow gotten themselves elected to "participate."

The cow manure was spread over the fields in early spring using a mechanical manure spreader. It was about fifteen feet long, four feet wide, and had a single axel with two large tires. It was hitched to the back of an old pickup truck. Overwintered and somewhat composted cow manure and straw was a very good nutrient and helped the grass and clover in the pastures to grow strong and tall. We referred to the smell that permeated the air for miles after it was spread as the "fresh-baked bread" fragrance. It usually caused the person you were talking to at the time to breathe in deeply when you mentioned "fresh-baked bread."

Chapter 17: Fresh-Baked Bread

We proceeded to explain the process to the new boys. "You throw the manure up on the back of the manure spreader using pitch forks. You have to watch for twine or you could get "twanged" by not only old manure but also fresh cow pies. It is the responsibility of an older boy to drive the pickup and back the manure spreader into position as we move further into the barn. Once the manure spreader is completely loaded, the older boy will head for the pasture and we five, not you three, will ride on the back of the pickup as our reward, while the manure is being spread."

This was an absolutely beautiful Saturday and none of us wanted to be in the barn forking manure. We all wanted to be outside. Once the manure spreader was loaded, Gilmer went up to the older kid driving the truck and talked to him a bit. He came back and said that we were ready to leave and that everyone except the new kids were to get on the back of the truck to go for a ride. It would take about half an hour.

The new kids started complaining that we had done this many times before and they had never had a chance to ride on the back of the truck. Hesitating for a while, we decided that they were making a good point. We told them to sit in the center of the bed of the truck and not to stand up at any time. They piled on eagerly, and we watched as they left.

Throughout our years at the Home, we were taught respect for elders, honesty, compassion, and a fierce loyalty to stand by the weak. But an inevitable mischievousness develops when you place a group of boys and girls together, even in a loving and compassionate environment like the Children's Home. It becomes an art form, and I must admit that in my case it has continued to grow throughout my sixty-eight years. We focus on doing no harm, but we see "experience" as a great teacher.

We knew it was the desire of these young lads to be treated fairly. No doubt about that. But we knew, in a silent communication between each of us older kids, that it was simply "the right thing to do" …!

As the old pickup truck pulled out of the barn and headed toward the north pasture, the three kids were ecstatic. We very calmly stuck our pitchforks into a small remaining pile of manure. Then after waiting a minute, which was like ten years in Children's Home boys' time, we ran like bats out of hell toward the north pasture, ducking and darting between barns, behind cows, and up to the top of a rise. Off in the distance, we could see the old pickup, the manure spreader, and the boys, the sweet young, innocent lads!

Once on top of the hill in the pasture, we saw the older boy driving the truck increase his speed to ten miles per hour, the perfect, and maximum allowed, delivery speed. Then he reached out and yanked on the rope to start the manure spreader.

The ride up the hill on a beautiful spring day was a treat. This wasn't as bad a day as it might have been, or was it? The boys felt the old pickup increase speed, sensed the soft spring breeze pick up, and smelled the wildflowers in bloom. It was a glorious day.

The rope pulled taunt, the lever engaged the steel chain, and the tines started to spin. As the tines spun, the steel chain lattice in the bed of the manure spreader ever so slowly moved back to deliver the manure into the tines. Then it started. Manure was thrown over twenty feet into the air out the back of the manure spreader. The boys watched as it lifted into the air and sailed freely, landing in a twenty-foot wide swath behind the spreader. The driver increased the speed to fifteen miles per hour, and the manure spreader started roaring into full action.

Eyes are funny. You can watch a person's eyes and tell a lot about the person and his or her mood. In this case, it was a dead giveaway. The "not recommended" fifteen miles an hour created the eighty-twenty rule. Eighty percent of the manure went out the back onto the pasture and, YES, twenty percent went straight up and then down into the bed of the truck – the driver told us that he could see the eyes of kids in the back of the truck getting as big as saucers.

As mentioned, some of the manure was fresh. Well, fresh manure had a tendency to be the twenty percent. You have never seen or heard such screaming in all your life. It wasn't from the lads on the back of the manure spreader; it was from us. We were hysterical with laughter. Even the good Lord was probably laughing.

This "consideration" guaranteed us a month of restriction, and every Saturday we were relegated to cleaning out the infamous ditch that the washdown from the milk room drained into. In addition, the driver was not permitted to drive again for a long while, and the young lads … well, let's just say that they would some day pass along this lesson.

Boys on a fishing trip.

Swamp Monsters

"Some of the chief considerations to be kept in mind in a project such as ours are the promotion of worth while work assignments, the furnishing of good school facilities and the providing of challenging play opportunities. Work and school assignments must be so directed and so evaluated as to appeal to youngsters. The work of each child is graded as his schoolwork is graded and a premium is put upon good endeavor, both as to the honorarium payments and other considerations. For instance, if a girl or boy does not break dishes in carrying them to or from the tables he is rewarded with a little extra pay. We have noted that reward for good services rendered serves the Home well economically, and, better than all that, it serves the child better psychologically. We proceed on the assumption that rewards for good service are better than penalties for poor services. However, we have both."

L ike most children, we were mesmerized with ghost stories. Occasionally, with the permission of the Home Mothers, one or two of the older boys would take a group of younger kids up to the gully, where the Children Home's dumpsite was, and set up a campfire. They would then cook hotdogs and later roast marshmallows. During this time they would learn to build campfires, share assorted tales and, as the late day grew into night, tell ghost stories.

It was a late-fall Saturday and Grady and I were heading to the upper pasture to have a cookout of our own. We had a flat piece of tin and two forks, along with a potato, two eggs, and some bread. We had gotten the food from the grocery store owner on Renolda Road near Georges Grill. George was an old man (to us), who had come over from Greece with his parents. His hotdogs were absolutely the best, and he proudly displayed his sanitation grade "C" for everyone to see. We thought it was the highest award you could get because his food was so good. Anyway, the grocery store owner was always helping us kids, and this was one of those times. After we helped him carry out trash and break down boxes, we got our reward. We used the two dollars to purchase our fixings. Off we went on yet another great adventure.

The upper pasture was only about a mile from the main campus if you took the long way around, but it was far enough removed to permit the adventure to be out of sight of all living things. We walked along the dusty dirt road leading toward the upper pasture and past the little white church. That was where Paula Ray was buried. She was a kid from the Home who had died from polio or something like that. This particular late afternoon, we chose to run past the graveyard and over into the upper pasture. However, if there were three or more boys, you would need to show your bravery and walk past the graveyard. But, on the inside, we were all running.

When we got to the upper pasture, we proceeded to set up our campfire. We gathered a few large rocks and a log to place on them to form a bench. We then gathered firewood, which consisted mostly of wet pine, and placed it in front of the log bench and put rocks on either side to rest the tin upon. We used dry leaves from a nearby tree to start the fire. By the time the fire was burning enough so it could be used for cooking, we were covered with smoke. Our faces were nearly black and our clothes were soot covered, as we had to continually blow on the embers to fan the fire. It wasn't a great success as fires go, but as it had gotten dark, it had a nice glow about it.

We were enjoying ourselves nonetheless, talking about twelve-year-old-boy things, including the occasional men-tion of a girl or two. When we ran out of local gossip, we started telling scary stories, each story getting increasingly more scary. Gradually, our attention moved toward the fact that it was quite dark, and our ghost stories were starting to get the best of us. Home boys can recognize any noise in the woods and pasture. The noise that we didn't recognize was cause for alarm, especially at night and in a place so far from civilization.

Grady was telling a story about a couple in a car and an escaped mental patient's arm hook on the car door handle when we heard a large thump in the dark distance. Not only was this noise unrecognizable, it was so loud that it shook the ground.

The hair stood up on the backs of our necks, and we jumped to our feet. Just then, the tin over the fire made a loud pop and we both bolted. Instinctively, we ran in the same direction, away from the loud thump and away from the fire, eggs, potato, and burnt toast. Before we realized it, we were near the little white church and the graveyard. The GRAVE YARD, and at night!!! We stopped dead in our tracks, our hearts pounding, as we were now feeding off each other's fear. Little by little we crept our way past the graveyard with every step seeming like forever, even if getting just a bit faster.

The terror of the ghost stories, the thump in the near dark, the gunshot-like sound from the cooking tin buckling under the heat, and now the graveyard. Our fear was nearly uncontrollable, and it was now totally dark. By the time we reached the other side of the graveyard, we were at a full "run for your life" speed, straight down the hill, across the creek, and through the briars. We had cut across the pasture and up toward the gully. From there we were going to head to the barns, leaving just a short sprint home. Both of us had ripped our shirts going through the briar patches. Blood was streaming from my face from a quick, yet hard encounter with a large rose bush. Neither of us wanted to be last, and neither of us was.

In the meantime, things were going along swell at the gully campfire. The two older kids in charge were at the height of their glee, telling ghost stories and watching the younger kids squirm and move closer to each other and the fire. They were just at the end of a particularly scary story about swamp monsters when the two older boys, on cue from each other, stood up and yelled to really scare the kids. This was going to be the culmination of the evening and was almost too funny to pull off without bursting out laughing. Just as they were standing up and were in a half-crouched position, they saw two fast-approaching shadows getting closer and closer. Then they saw the blackened, horror-filled faces, the blood, and the tattered clothes.

Chapter 18: Swamp Monsters

Grady and I were not expecting to see anyone at the gully. The kids blocked the fire from our view as it had burned down to embers. It was only when two crouching figures appeared immediately in front of us with the reflection of the embers against them that we realized that someone or something was there. It was too late to stop. Our momentum could not be controlled, and our state of mind would not allow it. We were overcome by fear and couldn't help yelling at the top of our voices. We ran right through the group, not realizing who or what was there.

Pandemonium immediately broke out around us. The older boys started yelling, and the younger kids all panicked. Everyone was running down toward the barns. No one took the road, everyone ran straight through the turnip field. The two older boys and kids blew by us, as their fear apparently exceeded ours.

At this very moment, Gilmer and Sam Vickory were coming out of the barn. Covered with straw from head to toe, they were shining their somewhat dim flashlights on each other and laughing at how silly they both looked. Needless to say, the sight of them in the ghoulish light just added to the kids' panic.

Now there were two groups of kids running and screaming. One group was on the right side of the barn and down the road to the boys' cottages, and the other group was on the left side of the barn and down the road leading past the farm manager's and dairy manager's homes. Gilmer and Sam just stood there yelling and running in place. Only then did Grady and I stop. We were so out of breath we thought we would die. Thank goodness I recognized that one of the ghouls was Gilmer.

After everyone had caught their breath, we told them of our adventures in the upper pasture. They commented on how we looked like we had been in a forest fire. We all cleaned up in the dairy milk room and headed home. My scratches were minor, and we were able to tuck in our shirts to look a bit less disheveled.

When we finally arrived back at the cottage, we were greeted with stories of how two bloody swamp monsters had nearly killed the kids up at the gully. No one thought to question the four of us, as there were only two swamp monsters. Several members of the staff were dispatched immediately to investigate. Nothing and no one was found, other than a scattered campfire, packages of hotdogs, marshmallows, and some shoes. One of the men drove into the upper pasture and found the remains of a campfire. It too was investigated but nothing was found except a piece of tin, a couple of raccoons, and a thirty-foot recently fallen, rotten tree.

The older boys and the kids did not recognize the swamp monsters, and they were never found. However, it was a very long time before anyone went to the gully for a cook-out at night. I can still see the sheer horror on the two older boys' faces as their eyes bugged out and they turned to run for their lives. It was everyone for themselves. I won't give up their names as they are still alive, but it is a sure bet that they will never forget the swamp monsters.

CHAPTER 19:

Bombs Bursting in Air

"We do not pretend to have attained any degree of perfection in the rearing of children in the institutional way, but we are dealing with the problem in a constructive way. Our efforts are earnestly used in an attempt to make our home life just as effective as possible. The chief asset in this effort is the type of personnel used. The next is the opportunity for the individual use of judgment on the part of the youngsters themselves. Constant deliberations and consultation are necessary in the functioning of these factors. While some mistakes are continually being made in our trial and error process, we like to point to the output of our youngsters as an evidence of the value of our undertaking."

Jerry Murdock, age 7, with cousin George Poole.

Chapter 19: Bombs Bursting in Air

Some movies make you want to run at the slightest hint of conflict or danger. Werewolf and Dracula movies come to mind as particularly scary. These would keep any teenager and most adults on the edge of their seats in the mid-1950s. But one movie scared everyone to the point of not wanting to go to sleep ... *The Body Snatchers*!! When you saw that movie, it made you want to walk in a group from the movie to home. After particularly frightening movies, somebody in the group was always elected to walk backwards to see if anyone or anything was following us and warn us accordingly.

In 1956 we were in our early teens. There was an awful lot to do in terms of chores, homework, and sports. Most of the kids I hung with were pushing the envelope a bit when it came to finding interesting things to do. We had caught most types of snakes, caught frogs, fished, hiked in the mountains, were members of the Scouts, and could tie just about any knot. We were expert on slingshots, marbles, and wild tales. I think we could recognize most bugs and could stretch the imagination to just the other side of believable.

It was a cold day in North Carolina terms with temperatures around twenty degrees. The one good thing was that it was Saturday. We were racking our brains to see if we could remember doing anything wrong that week that would put us to working in the mill that morning, or to working in the ditch that afternoon, or both. I had long ago learned that our idea of good was often far removed from the Home Mother's idea of good. That was usually reflected in our honorarium, or lack thereof. When it came to getting high marks for good behavior, Gilmer and I were usually on the bottom of the list. A couple of girls ended up on that side of the list as well, but we'll not mention their names, for now at least.

Sometimes I thought they kept Gilmer and me at the Home because they needed a couple of good examples of "bad example." Walter Lord, Winfred Hammer, and Sam Vickory were usually accorded that distinction as well. One time pictures were taken of a group of kids, including us. Each kid in the picture was named, but we were referred to as "and others." Suppose they may have been on to us?

Since we were a study in the kind of kid not to be, on occasion, we felt we had to live up to that awesome responsibility. This particular event took place over at the Winston Theater in Winston Salem. My brother Gilmer and I had been experimenting with making black powder and had it down to such a point that we could create a pretty good explosion. We even had powder that would burn either slow or fast. It still wasn't good enough to go pick a fight with Indians using muzzleloaders, but it was good enough for our purposes.

Our first successful experiment was to create a rocket that blasted off from the ball diamond wall just south of the John Neal Building. The rocket went well out of visual range, and we thought it was a huge success. In fact, it went all the way up past the upper pasture and embedded itself in the side of a new house nearby. The fire department later surmised that it was a piece of metal that had fallen from a plane. That was fine for the homeowner and those who saw the white streak in the night sky. However, there was still concern on campus about the large blast that had came from the direction of the baseball field. I don't think anyone ever tied the two events together. There was a considerable amount of smoke, but no one was seen around the area. Children's Home boys were a few of those blessed with the ability to become invisible, especially when three or fewer boys were involved.

Chapter 19: Bombs Bursting in Air

On this cold Saturday night we had fashioned a bomb from a tennis ball and about two rolls of black electrical tape. We had placed a fuse in it made from two cherry bomb fuses stuck together. Our practice shots up in the pasture worked out pretty well. We had timed it so the bomb would explode at a particular point above the ground. In this instance, we needed some "hang time" as there had to be a hero in the making. Gilmer and I had concocted a plan that was sure to make Walter Jones a bona fide hero to the girl of his dreams.

I don't recall her name, but I do remember later, around Valentine's Day, Walter ripping open the large decorated box at school containing a Valentine's card he had sent her. Apparently, the girl had found another true love the day before Valentine's. He grabbed the flowery, sweet-smelling card (he had doused it with some cheap after shave) and tore up the envelope. Then he wrote another girl's name on a second envelope we had and placed it back in the box.

We didn't bother to fix the box and didn't bother mentioning it to anyone. I do recall that the girl was surprised that Walter didn't send her a card. Fact is she wanted to get more than one card from different boys. Thanks to Gilmer and me, two other girls got several cards from different boys. It made for interesting times during the days following.

Okay, our plan was simple. Walter was to invite this dream girl of his life to the movie Saturday night. It was a particularly scary movie. I think it was *Invasion of the Body Snatchers*, deliberately chosen because it was the kind of movie where a girl would be looking for someone to hold on to. It was the perfect setup for Walter. To make things even more memorable, Gilmer and I would send up one of our homemade bombs, propelled from the finest of homemade slingshots. The idea was to send up the "he's going to be a hero bomb" just as the movie was letting out. By then, everyone would be at the end of frazzled nerves and already prone to panic. Walter would save the day by putting his jacket and himself over the girl of his dreams to protect her. It just couldn't get any better than that.

It was generally accepted where we grew up that the younger kids let the older folks leave the theater first. It was the considerate thing to do. Everyone was in his place. I was the trigger guy and Gilmer was the lookout and fuse lighter. Walter was in the movie theater with his "babe," and as far as we knew everything was going great. As Walter later told us, it couldn't have been better. His date was nearly in his lap by the end of the movie. But then, so was the guy on the other side of him.

Gilmer was standing in full view of the theater. Soon he came running toward me and yelled that the movie was letting out! He quickly whipped out matches and started to light the fuse. We were cold, and I was shaking a bit! While trying to hold the fuse so it wouldn't shake so much and Gilmer could light it, I broke off the extension. That meant that it would go off sooner than planned. It was the best we could do under the circumstances. Gilmer lit the fuse; I aimed high above the theater and fired. It went higher than expected. We ran!!

Walter was walking out of the theater behind the older folks, and quite proudly had his arm around his true love. She asked him if he was going to put on his coat as it was very cold outside. He said he would once they got outside. As they were walking out the theater doors into the lobby, Walter was preparing his maneuver. In his mind, he would throw his coat over her and hold her tight. This was going to be talked about for days!

Chapter 19: Bombs Bursting in Air

Just as he was going out the door, there was a huge explosion and a fireball more than a hundred and fifty feet above the older folks leaving the theater. Instant panic ensued. The older folks start screaming and stampeded back into the theater. Walter, being the gentleman that he was, had let his true love go through the outside door first. But as Walter started to exit, a crowd surged toward the door, sweeping his love to the side and trampling him. All he could see was the floor and all he could hear were screams of terror. Besides, his coat was torn from his grasp.

By the time Walter got to his feet, the girl of his dreams was nowhere to be found. The only thing he could find was his ripped and trampled coat. It had soda and popcorn mashed into it. This had not turned out as any of us had expected. The bomb had gone off about five seconds too soon, about the time the fuse extension would have given it if it hadn't broken off.

Unaware of all this, Gilmer and I were near the back entrance of the campus waiting for our hero to show up. We were sure that things had worked out perfectly because we heard the blast up high above the theater and heard the screaming. It was simply a matter of Walter adding the finishing touches.

It wasn't long before Walter showed up. He didn't have any lipstick on him; he wasn't with anyone, and he looked like he had been run over by a train. All he could say was "I got stomped." We decided not to go into detail with him at that point as we had a pretty clear picture of what had happened just by looking at him. It was shortly afterwards that Walter headed for the box containing the Valentine's Day card.

Walter was one of our best pals. He crossed over some time ago. We miss him.

Pop Woosley surrounded by Home kids.

CHAPTER 20:

Stampede

"Our challenge is to surround the children with such environment and such cultivation as will modify poor inherited tendencies and capitalize on good inherited tendencies. We have a wonderful opportunity to think about the debatable question as to whether inheritance plays a bigger part than environment in growing life.

The first concern in the direction of children is to secure good directors. Good leaders will in the run of time help youngsters turn from wrong ways to right ways. The importance of staff workers being able to co-operate with one another is clearly evident. Much common sense and careful discernment are needed to secure this. Our observation is that this good state of affairs is best guaranteed when frequent meetings for consultation and discussion are held. Most differences of opinion tend to vanish when there is a desire to discuss mooted questions with open frankness and charitable understanding.

The direction of our younger children, while requiring discernment and skill, does not as readily run into the disciplinary annoyances as the direction of the older children. As children become more willful and their range of activity is widened they create more opportunities for trial and error experiences. Sympathetic and understanding direction serves mighty well in such situations."

The Children's Home was renowned for its care and education of children. We were no different than any other children in the state. We were simply without parents who had the means to properly care for us. In most cases, it was due to conditions brought on by the depression, war, the death of one of the parents, and in rare cases, it was due to the death of both parents. The point is that we weren't known as much for being an "orphanage" as for being a children's home; thus, the name.

Our home was much the same as any home. The tables were larger to accommodate more kids, and the showers and dorms were larger. Like any family, assignments were given to every child based upon age and ability. The Home Mothers were tenured and had a great deal of experience acting as surrogate parents. Each had a quality about her that included compassion, common sense, and remarkable patience. Though they had no formal education in child care, such as degrees or certificates, we had total trust in and respect for them and learned much from them over the years. They were exceptional people during extraordinary times.

Chapter 20: Stampede

As we aged, we moved from cottage to cottage along with our peers. Girls' cottages were on the south end of the campus and boys' cottages were on the north end, closest to the dairy and farm. Moves would usually occur every two years. Though we moved to a different cottage and under the direction of another Home Mother, we still kept close contact with the Home Mothers we had before. The family simply expanded.

There were about 170 unsuspecting participants in this story and two instigators by the names of Gilmer and Graham Murdock. For quite some time, we had enjoyed horror movies at the theater in Winston. We usually went at night and always sat toward the back of the theater or up in the balcony. The balcony was where most of the smooching went on. I don't recall being there for that event personally but do know it was frequented by a couple of our acquaintances from high school.

On this particular night, it was hot by North Carolina standards, somewhere around eighty-five degrees, partly cloudy, and with a full moon. The humidity in the air and the wind picking up told us that a storm was brewing. We had hurried to the theater just in time to get into the last seats in the back of the balcony.

The theater was packed on this Saturday night as this was date night and *Dracula* was playing. Guys liked to take their dates to a scary movie as it shortcut a lot of positioning. During a particular scary scene, the girls would scream and huddle close to the boy next to them. I've even seen a boy or two huddle up to the boy next to them, only to realize too late what they had done. Of course, we were taking notes of this for future bargaining. In one case, a guy we knew started to snuggle up to the girl beside him, only to realize his girlfriend was on the other side of him. I think the loud sound of "get off me, you pig" pretty much describes the unsolicited emotion this move brought about.

The movie was every bit as scary as it had been advertised. I don't think there was a single guy in the house whose date hadn't about sat in his lap on at least a couple of occasions. When Dracula appeared behind someone in a flash, everyone would scream and the movie would fade to a bat flying off out through the window. It was building to a fever pitch.

It was at this time that Gilmer and I noticed the sound of thunder in the background. We heard it before anyone else because we were closest to the side of the building the storm was moving toward. The movie was panning in on Dracula's casket. Bats were near, and a storm was brewing. Lightning was flashing all around. The hero with the wooden stake was approaching the casket. Just as he slowly opened the casket, Gilmer opened a wide-mouth jar of large moths we had caught the night before up at the barn. They instantly flew toward the projector light and toward the movie screen.

There are some things even twins don't tell each other! What Gilmer didn't know was that I had caught two bats earlier in the day in the top of the silo and had put them in a small tin box with a lid. They had been quiet throughout the day as they were sleeping. With the dark of the theater and a sense of the approaching storm, they were starting to get active.

Just as Gilmer released the moths, I released the two bats. Like the moths, the bats did not hesitate and were off like a flash. By now, the storm had arrived in its full fury, both in the theater and outside. The moths headed toward the projector as Dracula, in his bat form, was entering behind the fellow opening the casket. Just as he opened the casket, there was a tremendous flash of lightning. That, combined with the crash of thunder in the movie, a crash of thunder outside, the bats and moths, highlighted in the projector and onto the screen, was just too much.

The frenzy started in the balcony as the moths darted up against the lens of the projector, blinding themselves and turning downward, causing them to skip off the moviegoers below. The bats were darting around trying to catch the moths, and popcorn and soda started flying everywhere as the moviegoers were going berserk. Dracula himself appeared in full on the screen, throwing open his cape and bearing his fangs just as lightening took out the power.

What had started as a great date night turned into a regular stampede – the only thing missing was the mooing of cattle. Chivalry be damned. There wasn't a single gallant man or boy in the theater. The front doors blew open from the air pushed ahead of the stampeding crowd. It was as if ghosts had been summoned to open them. The two caskets that had been placed in the theater lobby for effect just added to the panic.

Everybody was running out into the rain, directly to their rides. Those of us who didn't have rides, and who could brave the caskets, stayed in the lobby. I started asking what had happened as though we had just entered the scene. Gilmer had disappeared. I was listening to a pretty girl talking rapidly and was trying to calm her … enough to get her name. It appeared that some big and terrible things were in the theater and they had wings. "It was horrible," she said, on the verge of breaking into tears of fear.

It took a good half hour to get things calmed down. The movie had stopped because the power was out, but the dark and the storm continued to feed everyone's fear. Everybody seemed to be crowding in on each other. There were about sixty of us in the lobby. Gradually, people started to get a bit more relaxed. The lights came back on and the storm started to move on. We were given free popcorn from the manager. I was talking to the pretty girl and it was starting to turn out well. She said she was feeling better and had just begun to tell me her name, "It's …"

The low growling noise was what first caught my attention. Then everyone, in unison, stared at the casket next to the popcorn machine. The lid started to rise and a hand appeared through the crack. There was complete bedlam. Everybody, I mean everybody, ran out into the street. Parents were arriving to pick up their kids, but their kids were running past them, anything to get away!

What really happened became clear later. During the original stampede, Gilmer had crawled into one of the caskets, where he lay waiting for just the right moment to deliver the final blow. Not only did he scare the bejeezus out of the crowd, but the manager and concession workers were running at full speed, too. In the craziness all around, Gilmer was able to quickly blend into the stampede. We caught up to each other and headed home.

Apparently the moths found their way out through the front or side doors during the stampede and the bats followed. No one was ever able to determine the cause of the ruckus other than to blame it on the storm. I am convinced that many moviegoers from that night haven't seen a Dracula movie since. As for me, I enjoy them more than ever as they bring back great memories.

Chapter 20: Stampede

Looking back, I can honestly say that few, if any, kids had as much fun as Gilmer and I and our Home brothers and sisters. Every time I smell the sweet honeysuckle that grows outside our back door or stop to enjoy one of the many blooms on our magnolia trees in the back yard, I remember with great fondness our childhood and our many adventures. It was a slice of heaven!

Boys and girls canning tomatoes.

CHAPTER 21:

The Cannery

"There are so many accounts of cruel and heartrending incidents from day to day that one reads with deep satisfaction of any event showing that there is something of human heart left in the world. Two such incidents are recorded in this morning's paper. One comes out of Bedford, Indiana, and has to do with a young war mother, Mrs. Donna Blevins, and her five small children. Her husband died in 1946 from an ailment suffered while he was in the service, and her house was to be sold for taxes. When the auctioneer, Mark Boyd, began to call for bids, county auditor Donald Smith stepped to his side and announced that the property was occupied by a widow with five children and a very limited income. The auctioneer then called for bids, and there was an extended silence broken at length by the voice of the widow bidding $15. Without an instant's hesitation the auctioneer cried, 'And sold to Mrs. Blevins.'"

Blackberry Rain

It wasn't uncommon for us to can six thousand gallons of fruits and vegetables in any given year. We raised all our own crops, including grain crops for farm animals and vegetables for our own consumption. Included among the vegetables we canned were tomatoes, green beans, lima beans, butter beans, Crowder peas, black-eyed peas, corn, and green peas. We also canned apples and peaches. In addition, we raised turnips, collards, carrots, beets, okra, squash, watermelon, cantaloupe, and pumpkins. In short, we had excellent food throughout the year for all 400-plus Children's Home boys and girls.

The nice thing about growing up in North Carolina was the weather and the scenery, not to mention the gracious living. We were in the Piedmont region of the state, or the foothills of the Great Smoky Mountains. There weren't a lot of bugs or mosquitoes. I remember mostly cool evening breezes and sweet honeysuckle and rose fragrance-filled days. It was like honey dripping from the air. The men and boys were all gentlemen, and the girls and women were ladies of discerning taste and southern manners. Straw hats, bonnets, scarves, and handkerchiefs were the order of the day. The women talked so slow it was like drizzling honey over buttered biscuits.

When we canned, we identified what was in each can by placing a swatch of paint on top of the can; red for tomatoes, green for green beans, a smaller swatch of green for green peas, yellow for sweet corn, brown for Crowder peas, etc. My personal favorites were peaches, two yellow marks, and apples, two red marks. The peaches were delicious and were in very high demand.

Certain things were in high demand at the Children's Home, including stale cakes that the Merrita Bread Company hauled to the pigpen, watermelons in the bottom grounds at the off-campus property, and, of course, the canned peaches. Anything worth being on the "you just gotta have" list was usually locked up in a safe and secure area, or so far away that it was difficult to get to without a well-planned and coordinated effort.

There were four ways to get peaches. You could eat as many as you could stomach when you canned them; you could sneak a can away from the canning line when canning; you could borrow them from a kitchen pantry; or you could enjoy them by devising a special entry into the cannery where they were stored.

The art of acquiring peaches (notice I didn't say "stealing." Stealing was a serious offense, and getting caught brought the wrath of "hard labor on Saturdays" upon you as well as those suspected of being involved, which was pretty much all the guys we palled with) involved reducing the risk of being caught by increasing the numbers of possible acquirers. If you tried to remove a gallon of peaches from the canning line, those in the current canning process would all be punished. If you acquired a can from a pantry, those with kitchen duty were suspect and subject to punishment. But if you were able to reduce the storage inventory, it would be early summer of the next year before they would notice the inventory being off. That being the case, whom could they blame? After all, the staff was also known to relieve inventory on occasion for a special event such as "hey, I know where canned peaches are, so I'll go grab a can." Let's just say that the inventory worked on the accuracy of the word "approximately."

So the vote was biased toward the least possibility of blame pointing toward us, and that meant acquiring them from storage. The difficulty of acquiring peaches from the cannery storage was twofold: how to get in and the time it would take. Each time we visited the cannery storage to get canned goods for the various kitchens on campus, we carefully surveyed the area, including ceiling, walls, and floor. We finally determined that the best way into the storage was through the floor in the back storage room. It permitted us to stay low and out of sight, and it allowed us to perfect the entry over a period of time, as the entry had to go undetected long after the event. And in standard tradition, we always posted a lookout who would signal should anything unusual be seen to be afoot. This normally was a whistle.

For three straight evenings in the winter of 1956/57, Walter Jones, Winfred Hammer, Grady Lord, Gilmer, and I snuck away from the other kids during free time and went to the cannery, spending about an hour each trip. We crawled beneath it on our backs. We had to use a flashlight, as it was dark. This was our greatest risk because of the possibility of the light being seen. We were able to pry up the floor in a spot where three one-by-four inch boards met in parallel at the floor joist. We had cautiously moved cans over a period of weeks during authorized and escorted visits to locate just the right spot. Also, we didn't want to try and lift boards covered with several hundred pounds of filled cans. All we needed to do was lift them enough to allow one person up into the cannery. We could then pull the nails from the boards in two spots, which would permit them to lay flat again once we left.

Winfred was elected to go into the opening, as he was the thinnest. As suspected, he was able to squeeze through. We ever so quietly edged the nails out. Winfred handed the hammer and nails down to us. The three boards lay back down perfectly. Everything was going just as planned.

Chapter 21: The Cannery

Meanwhile, unbeknownst to us, several of the older boys had decided that this particular Saturday evening they would take a joy ride in the dairy truck. They had pushed it up toward the upper barn and out the gate into the pasture. As always, they had posted a lookout. In fact, they had posted two lookouts, mainly because there wasn't room enough for everyone in the truck.

It was dark in the cannery and Winfred didn't have a flashlight. We held the boards up while he fumbled in the dark for the peaches. Soon he handed a gallon through the hole. It was a sheer joy to finally have received our reward for such marvelous planning and cunning, not to mention the patience of three days' work.

The first whistle absolutely startled us. All of a sudden Walter came sliding under the cannery, panic stricken. "Who whistled?" he asked in a panicked voice, "who whistled??" It wasn't one of us. The sound was somewhat faint and had to come from someone trying to warn us, but no one else knew of our plans, or did they?

Panic set in. We crawled out as fast as we could, leaving the can of peaches underneath the cannery. Once out, we ran toward the woods and then home, but suddenly we realized Winfred wasn't with us. He must still be in the cannery, we figured. Gilmer and I turned to go back and told Walter and Grady to mix back into the crowd and cover for us if need be.

Gilmer and I darted back under the cannery. Winfred was in a real jam. He couldn't pry the floor up because he didn't have any tools and didn't have a flashlight. His heart was in his throat, as he knew he was about to get caught. We heard him desperately scratching around for the loose boards. To help, we raised the boards under his knees, scaring him half to death. He flew through the hole. Then we quickly pulled the boards back down, grabbed the gallon of peaches, and took off like scared rabbits.

As we each mingled back into the goings-on, we were soon called to line up for a head count. Coach Clary and our Home Mother were looking us all over. Every one of the five of us was petrified, as we knew the punishment would be long and severe. We wouldn't see a free Saturday again for six months. But since each of the twenty or so boys was accounted for, Coach Clary left. Our hearts settled down and we started to breathe again.

We weren't sure what had happened so we didn't say a word. In fact, we didn't talk to each other the rest of the evening and night. Sunday morning, we were sure that we would be asked to step forward. Breakfast passed and no word. Church was over and no word. Finally, at lunch when everyone was in the dining room, the Home Mother came in and asked for everyone's attention. We just about died. Walter asked to be excused, but the Home Mother told him to stand where he was. She then started in. "Last night, several of our boys, whom we had trusted, did something very wrong. They"… Winfred could hold it in no longer. He jumped up and shouted that he wasn't the only one, that "Walter Jones, Grady Lord, and the Murdock twins were in on it with me." Miss Cottle looked stunned and said. "I didn't know you boys were in on the joy ride, too!!!! I didn't even know you knew how to drive, Winfred??"

Holy cow! It wasn't about the cannery and the peaches, but it was soon to be if Winfred was allowed to continue unchecked. Gilmer jumped to his feet and said, "That's right, Miss Cottle, we were the ones who short-sheeted Miss Reynolds. We knew it was wrong and we apologize." Miss

Chapter 21: The Cannery

Cottle said, "It's not about that and we don't have time for your tom-foolery, Gilmer. Sit down ... all of you." By this time, we were all near death. Winfred was about to fess up to something we did but hadn't been caught doing. And he also nearly implicated us in something we didn't do.

Turns out that two of the older boys had been caught driving the dairy truck in the upper pasture. As luck would have it, they hit a log that was lying in the middle of the pasture and the truck got stuck on it. They were in the process of trying to get the truck off the log when they got caught. There was some suspicion that others were involved but they weren't caught and the two older boys denied anyone else was involved.

It was several days before we were able to get to the peaches. We arrived together at the place where we had hastily hidden them. There they were upside-down in the leaves next to a tree, just where we left them. These were going to be delicious. Walter reached down, can opener ready, and flipped them over. There it was in plain sight, the prettiest green mark you could ever want to see. GREEN!!!!!! We had acquired ... no ... stolen ... a can of GREEN BEANS!!!

That was the last time we looked for peaches in the dark. In fact, we never did go back to the cannery for peaches. None of us had the stomach for it after that episode. We left the green beans next to the door of a rundown house across the way. Figured they could use it. Left them the opener, too.

Everyone gathered for the watermelon feast.

CHAPTER 22:

Birthday Party

"Years ago we used to want to take issue with those who berated the bringing up of children in child caring institutions. Instead we found ourselves examining our program of direction to see if we were developing youngsters of pleasing personality and assuring dependability. In the run of years we have noticed that youngsters going out of our institutions in the area we know about, offer plenty of assurance that child caring institutions with constructive programs of service and direction, can and do a good job at raising children."

Most schools have a slogan that identifies the spirit of the school teams. Ours was Fighting Methodists. I think those that chose this title thought it represented our team psyche, team spirit, campus attitude, etc. In our case, it was probably all of these because we were very, very competitive and had strong team spirit.

We were at the Children's Home from 1947 through most of 1959, a solid twelve years. These were our development years and defined quite well who we would become. I can say with conviction that I am pleased with the results. If happiness is any measure, it has been a great success to date.

During the time we were there, there was on average 425 to nearly 500 boys and girls, ranging in ages from one year old to eighteen years old, though the youngest and oldest noted here were generally the exception. The vast majority of the kids stayed through graduation from high school. We were fortunate to have around twenty-five boys and a similar number of girls in our age group. We were long-term residents of the Children's Home family and became like brothers and sisters to each other.

In the fall of approximately 1956, we were engaged in one of our championship football seasons. Our record was excellent, and we were leading in our conference. It was a rare occasion when we were able to watch other teams play. The new conference rules had gone into effect, and we were restricted to play with teams representative of our size of school. We used to play the largest high schools and beat them regularly. On this particular day, our high school, Richard J. Reynolds High School, was playing Gray High School. Both schools were Triple-A schools and cross-town rivals. Both had excellent teams and supportive student bodies. This was a game we wanted to see.

Chapter 22: Birthday Party

It was a privilege to be able to leave campus on your own. The rules were simple: Stay out of trouble, stay safe, and return on time. The fact that you were able to get past being restricted was a feat in itself, so this was a no-brainer. Any time a Murdock could get through a week without getting caught doing something wrong usually meant that the staff just wasn't paying attention. After all, how could we otherwise have been having all this fun?

Gilmer and I were looking for a way to get to the Gray-Reynolds game that Saturday evening. It was across town and too far to walk. We had to find a ride and needed someone to go with us to increase the fun quotient. What good is having fun if you can't share it? We got in touch with just about everyone, but they all had other plans.

We finally cornered Walter Jones and Grady Lord and asked them to join us. But they said that they were busy ... something about a hornet's nest. We told them we would go with them to get the hornet's nest if they would go with us to the game. They agreed, but we were still left with the task of arranging for a ride for all of us to the game.

In casting about for ideas, I remembered a student at Reynolds High in the tenth grade with me who had always wanted a date. Up until now, I had put her off. She had a car, among other things, such as a pool, a tennis court, and a butler. I snuck into the Home Mother's room at John Neal, where we lived, and called her. She was delighted to hear from me, and I found out that she had not yet made plans. This girl was so homely that plans of any kind were simply avoiding her. Gosh, I learned not to judge on looks, and shouldn't. She was actually very nice, as we found out later. At any rate, Charlotte was to pick us up at 7:00 p.m. at the south campus entrance.

Blackberry Rain

Before the appointed time, Walter, Grady, Gilmer, and I set out for the hornet's nest. This thing was huge. The last time we had seen it, it was big, but it had somehow gotten much bigger. In fact, it was so big that we all wondered just what we could do with it. We had brought a small hatchet used for Scout camping trips, but we had to get a sack. Off Walter went to the mill to grab a feed sack. We also needed something to tie the sack with, and tape to close the hornet nest's entry/exit hole. Off went Grady to scrounge up some rope. He got it from the laundry of all places and also brought back some clear tape. Now it was a simple matter of putting the hornet's nest into the sack. We had to do this without getting stung! Where was Winfred Hammer when you needed him? He was an expert at this type of thing.

Hornets are mean and suspicious. I think sometimes they sting just for the joy of it. We had to avoid getting stung at all costs and that would take speed and agility. A hornet's sting swells fast and is very painful.

Unfortunately, this nest was quite high up in the tree. The one good thing was that it was attached to a relatively small limb that was pretty easy to reach. Up the tree I went. Gilmer and Walter were the bag guys, and Grady was to pace back and forth, at least that's what he did. I think he was more nervous than I was.

I was able to get up the tree and to the limb supporting the nest. The fact that it was a sizable tree helped keep it from moving while I climbed. Boy, there were a lot of hornets. In and out, in and out; they were busy. I had one shot at the limb with the small hatchet. I removed the hatchet from my belt. The first whack had to do it, or there was going to be hell to pay. WHACK! WHACK!! It took two rapid chops to free the limb. Down it went! Lucky for me, the hornets didn't have time to rush out after the first whack.

Walter and Gilmer were at the bottom of the tree trying to catch the nest. Since it was attached to a limb, it was not going to be easy to get into the sack. Fortunately, the nest was heavy so its momentum caused it to fall through the branches below. As the end of the limb hit the ground with a thud, Walter and Gilmer ran over and placed the sack over the nest. They could hear the hornets buzzing frantically in the sack. There was no time to tape over the hole. They yelled for me to throw down the hatchet so they could cut the limb off each side of the top of the nest. Then they pushed the nest into the sack, wrapped the rope around the top of the sack and held the top tight. Boy ... those hornets were mad.

I scurried down the tree as fast as I could. The hornets returning to the nest were flying all around the area up in the tree and started scouting toward us. We ran!!

Now we had to decide what to do with the nest. It was too dangerous to carry because the hornets could sting through the sack. We had to put the sack in a box. We found a suitable box outside the back door of the dining room by the trash. As we put the sack in the box, the rope we had wrapped around the top loosened, so we quickly taped the box closed. The dark appeared to settle the hornets; at least we couldn't hear them. But we still weren't sure what to do with them.

At that point, we realized it was about 6:30. We had less than half an hour to get cleaned up and meet Charlotte down by the back campus gate. That's when we decided to bring the nest with us. We would put it in Gray High School football team's dressing room. What an ingenious idea. Since we all attended Richard J. Reynolds High, we knew the team pretty well. We would add a bit of additional support to their effort to beat Gray High.

Charlotte was on time, just as she promised. She was driving a huge Buick that could hold nearly a thousand people, it seemed. She was wearing a perfume that said, "Run for your life." Man, it was strong! We all got in the back seat, with the box on Walter's lap. Charlotte turned around and looked back at me, and I knew that I had to ride up front with her, so I opened the back door and moved up front. In the meantime, Walter set the box on the seat I had vacated. He had wrapped paper over it in an effort to deaden any sound. Apparently, Christmas wrapping was all he could find. "What's in the box?" Charlotte asked. We explained that it was a football helmet one of the girls had painted initials on for one of the Reynolds football team members. This was the usual fast thinking that one could expect from Home boys. It was one of our survival techniques – that and being able to become invisible.

Off we went to the ball game. The one thing we hadn't given any thought was Charlotte's driving ability. Also, we didn't know why she wore thick glasses. It soon was revealed to us: She was nearly legally blind. She came within a hair of plowing the car in into trees as well as other cars. It was a harrowing ride. Add this to her looks, and you could readily see why she had so much free social time. To make matters worse, she talked nervously the entire time. But hey, even this beat walking – although by a very, very narrow margin.

As we approached the stadium, we asked Charlotte to park near the back of the bleachers so we could avoid all the traffic after the game was over. We directed her toward the closest entrance to the Gray High locker room. The idea was to leave the box in the car until toward the end of first half. We would then slip it into the dressing room and put it conspicuously in the center of the room. A great plan, if I must say so myself. However, Charlotte insisted that it be delivered immediately and signaled a parking attendant over. She gave him a few bucks and told him to deliver the box immediately and put it in the locker room Gilmer and I pointed out to him. That was the way she and her family did things, by having someone else do them. We were not in a position to protest.

It was a tough-fought football game. At the end of the first half, the score was seven to six with Gray in the lead. Just prior to the first half break, we edged our way toward the end of the field near the lockers. The first half ended, and everyone headed toward the locker rooms. We could hardly wait. But we did! We waited … and waited … and waited … Nothing happened. Absolutely nothing! Finally, the second half started. We were terribly disappointed. There was no way to check things out, as there were too many people around the area. The game ended with a tie.

We got back into the car. Charlotte wanted to go to her house to shoot pool, so we agreed. We told her we needed to be home by eleven. It was now about 9:30 p.m. Off we went, driving like we were blind. At one point, Charlotte looked back laughing at something one of the guys had said. Ever so slowly we veered left into oncoming traffic. I yelled, but it was too late. We hit a pickup truck.

Had it not been for the fact that we were in a tank, and the fact that the truck was able to slow down, it would have been a bad accident. As it was, all of us were just fine but the driver of the truck had hit the steering wheel. His forehead was bleeding quite badly. An ambulance was dispatched, and Charlotte insisted that we go with him to the hospital. Since there was little damage to her car, we followed the ambulance. Thankfully, Baptist Hospital wasn't far from the Home, so at least we were going in the right direction.

The driver of the pickup, a guy just a bit older than us, required six stitches. Other than that he was fine. His friend, who had been riding in the truck with him, was able to drive their truck as it had only sustained a crumpled bumper.

On our way out the door, we saw a commotion in the emergency room lobby. Four boys yelling and fighting with each other. Their parents were just arriving, and the mothers were hollering back and forth. Turns out, according to the boys, they were at a friend's birthday party and somebody had left a large gift on the table. When their friend opened it, there was a hornet's nest full of hornets!! They were all covered with stings and blaming each other. Upon closer inspection, we could see, through a swollen face, that one of the boys was the parking attendant. They weren't at a birthday party. They had stolen what appeared to them to be a gift – and what a gift it turned out to be. Apparently, they had opened it in their car and were unable to escape in time. We overheard one of the nurses saying that one boy had eighteen stings. The others had about as many, and they were plenty painful. At least, had the box been opened in the locker room, the football equipment would have given some protection. Not much, but some!!

Our disappointment turned to utter delight and laughter once we got outside. It hadn't worked as we planned, but it worked in a way that no doubt corrected the life's course of some would-be thieves. We didn't share the story with Charlotte, as we weren't sure she would understand. It had gotten too late to play pool, but she did run us by Bowman Dairy for ice cream before dropping us off. She said she had enjoyed the evening and looked forward to seeing us again.

Charlotte developed into quite a beautiful lady. Our occasional talks at Reynolds High were enjoyable. Little by little, her confidence blossomed. The last time I heard from her, she had graduated from Duke as a doctor. Don't know if she ever learned to drive well, but we hope so!!

As for us boys, let's just say the adventures continued. I don't know of any kids who pushed the envelope quite as far as we did. Boys and girls alike at the Home were continuing to show their individuality. We were blessed to be part of it.

Straw shed and silo.

Lower dairy barn.

CHAPTER 23:

The Silo Event

"We expect to widen the gates into our barn lot. We found this summer that the ten-foot gate was not wide enough to bring in the big trailers loaded with soybean hay. We have found this fall that the twelve-foot gate was not wide enough to bring in the tall silage corn that grew so luxuriantly. Thanks to a good season and careful cultivation, only about two-thirds of our silage corn was needed to fill and re-fill the three big silos. The farm crew has done a good job this summer and our barns are filled with what it takes to make the cows contented and their milk to flow bountifully."

Blackberry Rain

There were good days and there were great days at the Children's Home. Looking back, I honestly don't remember too many days that I would just as soon forget.

It was some time in late fall around 1956. The days and seasons seemed to run together. We were always busy and had school, sports, and chores ahead of us at all times. Since our time and activities were so well managed, it would appear to be impossible to have unsupervised activities. But like most children of adventure, we managed to find the opportunity to explore and test the boundaries of reason and common sense.

Most of our adventures outside supervision occurred on Saturdays or at night when we were supposed to be in our rooms asleep. However, there were also times between "responsibility handoffs" that presented opportunities for us to sneak away. A case in point was when a group of us was asked if we wanted to go to a ball game with one of the coaches or to go hiking, pick apples, etc. Usually it was a spontaneous event, and no one really kept a list of who was going or who was staying behind. It was as if a door of opportunity opened before us through which we could step out for unsupervised activity.

It was the middle of the week on a teacher conference day at Richard J. Reynolds High School. That meant it was a free day for the students. Usually, this annual fall day was used to get the boys and girls at the Home fitted for shoes or clothes, get shots, visit the dentist, or unload coal or tobacco stems from the rail car south of the campus. The coal was used to fire all the furnaces on campus, and the tobacco stems were spread over the pastures as a supplemental source of fertilizer. (No, you couldn't smoke them. We all tried at some point and nearly died as a result.)

Chapter 23: The Silo Event

There was something planned. And if there wasn't, we would most likely have football practice or be assigned to help at the dairy, the big farm, or the truck farm.

Work at the dairy included a number of chores. There was milking, of course, which was done twice a day at 3:00 a.m. and 3:00 p.m., feeding the cows after each milking, bedding them down in the colder months with straw from the straw barn, moving them from pasture to pasture, and cleaning out the barns in the spring.

When cleaning manure out of the barns, you would get it on you. Everyone would get into their work more than they wanted. Those bedding down the cows were very conscientious about keeping the twine picked up so the cows would not get caught in it and trip. Every now and then, one would slip by. We all paid dearly for it. We used pitchforks to load the manure onto a manure spreader. Sometimes there would be a "twanger." This was when you were getting ready to dump a load of manure onto the spreader and your pitchfork would be caught in mid-air by a piece of bailing twine that was entwined in the manure on the floor. The sudden jerk would cause the pitchfork to make a twanging sound and throw manure all over everyone.

There were a number of things involved in feeding the cows. You needed to read their chart to see how much ground feed to give each, cotton seed if required, and a supply of hay and silage. Silage consisted of the green corn stalk and ear ground up and put into the silo with a conveyer system.

Throwing silage down from the silo to feed the cows wasn't difficult, but to do so you had to climb up on the outside of the silo in an enclosed area using rungs that were much like a ladder. You climbed to just above the last of up to twenty-two boarded openings. The greatest problem was the many pigeons that roosted at the top of the silo, especially the one at the upper barn where the beef cows were. They would bomb us every day with their droppings just as we started up the rungs. We tried to scare them off before we started our climb, but it didn't always work. To protect ourselves, we put a sack on our heads before we started to climb, never looking up. About midway up, we could drop the sack because by then the pigeons had scattered. When we got down, we had to scrub our hands carefully since the rungs were usually splattered with droppings.

This particular day had been planned well in advance. Walter Jones, Bill Dobner, Grady Lord, and I were going to exact justice on the pigeons that had bombarded us for as long as we could remember. It was war!

The first order of business was to sneak away, individually, and then join up later at the dairy. As luck would have it, Coach Gibson was rounding up volunteers to pick apples. A friend of the Children's Home had an apple orchard near Waynesville, about seventy miles away, where we were allowed to gather all the apples that had fallen off the trees. Though some were rotten, many were in great shape, and we used them for applesauce, apple butter, and pies. We usually got about fifteen to twenty bushels.

This was one of those days when a door opened through which we could slip into "unsupervised" activity. Soon the bus left with about fifteen boys on board to go apple picking. We took full advantage of it and met up as planned by the dairy milk room.

Grady had gotten a couple of cherry bombs from a friend, who had gotten them from a friend, etc. The mere fact that you had and could hide such a trophy as a cherry bomb elevated you to "best friend" status for as long as you had it. In this case, Grady was already our best friend, among several others. We were going to shoot the cherry bombs up into the silo opening and time them to explode just as they hit the opening. The blast and echo would be horrendous. The pigeons wouldn't know what hit them.

It wasn't as simple as all that. We had a couple of things to consider. One was the angle we needed in order to hit the opening of the silo. The other was a place to hide after the blast. The straw barn solved both problems. It allowed the perfect angle and was a great place to hide, as it was exactly across from the upper barn and silo.

Bill Dobner volunteered to shoot the cherry bombs. Actually, he insisted since it was his slingshot. We managed a couple of practice rocks through the open window in the top of the silo. It scared the pigeons a bit, but they simply flew back into the silo.

It was time. We were standing at the edge of the straw barn under the roof overhang. Bill put a cherry bomb into the pocket of the slingshot. Grady lit it, and Bill pulled back on the slingshot. But just as he let go, the rubber on the slingshot snapped in two! The cherry bomb hit the underside of the roof in the straw barn and ricocheted back at us, hitting the ground right at our feet. Absolute panic set in. Before we could take as much as three steps, it exploded. Straw and dirt was flowing in all directions. Walter dropped the second cherry bomb.

As the dust started to clear, we realized that the straw at the edge of the barn had caught fire. We started stomping it as fast as we could. It was then that we realized that fire had also started behind us in the center of the barn and the fuse on the second cherry bomb that Walter had just dropped had lit. Everybody ran. Once again the famous Home motto of "all for one and one for all" was but a rumor, an imagination. Home kids stuck together when it came to situations outside the Home, but we were more prone to quick decisions related to events where only the Home kids were involved. In short, we weren't afraid to panic and could do so with great bravery, as in "we bravely ran away."

The explosion of the second cherry bomb was quite pronounced since it took place inside the tin barn. Shortly after it exploded, it blew burning straw up into the center of the barn with a deafening sound. This was a time when we all became invisible. As mentioned, Home boys and girls were blessed with the ability to become invisible during certain spirited times. It was also true that on occasion, Home Mothers and some staff could see invisible kids. Our hope was that we had the edge on this day.

The next thing I remember is that Walter and I were in the top of a large oak tree down past the milk barn. Our hearts were pounding so loud and hard that we thought we were going to die. Perhaps a far worse fate awaited us: We could be caught! Neither of us remembered running to the oak tree, nor did we remember climbing it. We thought only Winfred Hope and Bud Barnette were that skilled as they both were expert climbers. The panic finally started to subside and we regained some sense of where we were. We found ourselves high in the tree trying desperately to look like part of it for the better part of an hour.

Bill and Grady had disappeared into thin air. After the second explosion, everything was a blur. To this day, I vaguely recall Grady levitating off the ground. Bill looked like a ball of dust as he headed north, out of the barn. Wherever they went to hide was very effective as we could see a long way in all directions and never caught a glimpse of them. I recall seeing B. L. Angel, the farm manager, pulling the manure spreader away from the side of the barn. What it normally took two horses or a pickup to pull, he managed to do easily himself. He was the first one summoned to the barn by the loud blasts and then the plume of smoke. He promptly called the fire department.

From the tree, Walter and I watched as the fire engine from town buzzed by in its own cloud of dust. All they could do was contain the fire. The straw barn was too far gone by then to be saved. The flames from the fire reached well into the sky. It was awesome! A large crowd of kids and adults gathered by the dairy. Walter and I used this opportunity to slowly weasel our way down and joined the crowd of kids watching the fire. No one knew how it started, but there were assurances of an investigation.

This became another of the many "mysteries" at the Home. In true fashion, no one ever told of the silo, the pigeons, or the "plan." In fact, I don't think Dr. Perry Lefeavers included the burning straw barn in his book, *The Children's Home, The First Seventy-Five Years*. It was something best left untold.

I don't know what it was, but to this day I swear we could hear pigeons laughing at us. No wonder, it must have been one funny sight from where they were sitting – four boys trying desperately to stomp out a fire and soon thereafter a second cherry bomb going off!

To my knowledge, this is the first time anyone has divulged this story. But then again, the angels in our midst at the

Home knew and decided not to tell! After all, we were blessed kids.

Our adventures at the Children's Home continued for several more years. As time went by and we left the Home, we lost personal contact with many of our friends, but they never left our hearts and minds. I recall with fondness their friendships, and from time to time remember another of our many adventures. In recent years, we have attended the annual Homecoming and walked the paths of the past, visiting with our many Home brothers and sisters. I can recall the many good times we had and still hear the distant laughter. It reminds me of a song we grew up singing quite often:

"Row, row, row your boat gently down the stream, merrily, merrily, merrily, merrily, life is but a dream."

Girls stringing beans.

Appendix

Pop Woosley with senior girls and their Home Mother.

Special Influences
in Our Lives

As noted previously, the stories in this collection were written from two boys' perspectives but could be echoed by most of the other boys and girls, replaced with the names of their Home Mothers, teachers, and other influences.

In addition to our families of origin, there were many special influences in our lives when we were growing up. They were the Home Mothers, the teachers, the farm and dairy staff, and wonderful Mom and Pop Woosley, the superintendent and his loving wife. We called them Mom and Pop out of a genuine and abiding love, not because we had to call them that.

Looking back, it is hard to imagine how Home Mothers like Miss Carter, Mrs. Reynolds, Miss Little, Mrs. Shifford, Mrs. Ammons, the unforgettable Tula Harrison, Miss Harmon, and Miss Byrd at the main dining hall had the incredible patience to hang in there with us boys. There was also Miss Holland, one of the cooks, who always offered guidance and uttered never a cross word, and Miss Smith, the nurse at the infirmary, who helped ensure we healed properly when we were sick or hurt. What wonderful, patient, and caring saints.

The truck farm and the big farm added a great deal to help shape our character. Paul Booze ran the truck farm with the help of Mr. Heggie, and our dear friend Johnny Horton. Some of us actually learned the difference between a weed and a vegetable. I'll never forget how meticulous one of our classmates, Talmadge Lane, was about making his neat rows. Once Johnny Horton, one of the farm hands, pointed out to Talmadge that he had done a nice job; however, Talmadge needed to get a better understanding of the difference between a weed and a tomato. He had cut down a row of tomatoes and nicely lined out a row of weeds. After replanting the row, we all paid a bit more attention.

Another standout was Dad Shaver, who was in charge of our award-winning dairy. He was always teaching us something, and was ever ready to lend a helping hand. I don't recall ever hearing a harsh word from him. He was the one who would fill in for you if you wanted a weekend off. It is for good reason that he was called "Dad Shaver."

B. L. Angell ran the big farm. He was an accomplished farmer and a strong mentor. He always honked his horn as he approached the pigpen the day Merrita Bread dropped off their stale bread and cakes. He delighted in seeing the boys who were secretly stealing cakes pour from the pig barn and run for the creek. Sometimes he would sit and wait for everyone to swing off the roof and into the barn where the bread and cakes were, and then he would hit the horn. It was like rats fleeing a fire.

Eddie Newsome helped keep the campus looking like a pristine sanctuary, with well-manicured lawns and beautifully trimmed bushes. We often referred to him as "The Shadow" as he was forever scaring half the life out of you when you were sneaking off at night up to no good. Eddie was a skilled photographer. He helped all the kids.

Special Influences in Our Lives

Gray Todd probably knew more of what was happening around campus than anyone; yet, he never told a soul. Many a day he could have cost us dearly, but instead of telling on us, he would simply suggest that we consider the options and that was that. We tried hard not to lose his trust. Gray made the Christmas tree at the entrance to the campus a highlight each year. Every Homecoming, we looked for Gray so we could say hello. He was a strong and positive influence on us all.

There were other significant influences in our day-to-day lives.

Coach Clary was a great coach, who challenged us to do our best at all times. He instilled the "never let up" attitude in each of us. Coach Clary was always teaching us the value of hard work. He constantly reminded us to do a good day's work and see how good it felt when it was accomplished. He was always there to talk if you needed advice.

Coach Edwards was probably one of the most diplomatic people I know. He would help us work through problems and was a great coach. He always made you feel like a winner and had some great anecdotal stories. I also enjoyed him as principal and a Sunday school teacher.

Coach Gibson was a great leader, a wonderful teacher, and a tenacious fighter. He played to win and loved to see a game plan work well. He was always available to help and was a great Scout leader. When you saw him coming, you knew there was adventure and fun in store.

There were rumors that Miss Dinkens, my first "favorite English teacher," was the hardest teacher that ever lived. I recall that we all feared the day when we moved up to her class. Only after I left the Home did I appreciate the education she gave each and every one of us.

Blackberry Rain

When I moved up to Reynolds High School, my second "favorite English teacher" was Miss Lillian Rhodes. I swear I think she was related to Miss Dinkens. She was demanding and did not let anything escape her. When you left her class, you knew how to diagram any sentence in the world. She taught us the meaning of a sentence, the implied meaning of a sentence, the hidden meaning of a sentence, and what wasn't said and the meaning of that. I believe to this day she could read thoughts. I think this was when I learned the art of never making eye contact unless I wanted to have a conversation with someone.

Of course, there were everybody's favorites … Mom and Pop Woosley. They were the essence of the Children's Home. They worked hard every day to see that each and every child was taken care of. They knew every child by name, and every time they walked around the campus they looked like Pied Pipers, with kids following them. Everyone trusted them, and everyone loved them deeply.

I don't doubt for one moment that each of these folks has or will have a pair of wings waiting for them. God bless them all, and God bless the Children's Home.

Things We Never Discussed
at the Home

It wasn't that we were forbidden to discuss certain things. It was simply that we weren't encouraged to do so.

We did not disparage other people's religion. It wasn't until we joined the Marines that we encountered religions not of the Protestant faith. Catholics in the Corp went to mass, ate fish on Friday, and put ashes on their foreheads. We still don't see the difference religion makes, unless it is used as a means to destroy.

The use of words to describe, in a derogatory manner, a person of another race was not prevalent at the Home, contrary to what some would have you believe. We referred to blacks only as "colored" because that was what the sign over bathrooms and drinking fountains said in those days. I clearly remember the first "colored" girl to attend Richard J. Reynolds High School. She was very nice. The first day she attended caused quite a scene. We were told to avoid the crowds and the press. After a while no one really paid much attention because we had more important teenage things to do.

At the Home, one of our favorite staff was a "colored" man named Johnny Horton, who worked as a hired hand on the truck farm. He was great to us kids, and never ever had a harsh thing to say. During blackberry season, we would go with Johnny Horton to the blackberry patches on the land the Home owned in the river bottoms. The two other truck farm supervisors went along. Each boy was given a gallon can and sent into the blackberry patch to pick berries ... and get a heavy dose of chiggers. Though there were berry patches in the pastures at the Home, they weren't big enough for us all to pick.

After a couple of hours of picking, we were called over to the truck and had to hand in our blackberries. We always hid two gallons and snuck them into Johnny Horton's truck. They were the biggest and ripest. The other staff never knew. When we got home, we washed with an alcohol-soaked rag, especially the important parts.

There was and is always the potential for the presence of child abuse or child molesters in surroundings where there are lots of children. At the Children's Home, staff probably queried the kids about that sort of thing on an ongoing basis. It's just that they did it with great finesse. I don't recall ever having that type of conversation; however, I do recall that we were taught to let our Home Mothers know of all strangers on the campus. To our knowledge, abuse of this kind was never a problem at the Home. If cases occurred, they were handled quietly and quickly through a zero tolerance mandate.

There were never any discussions about gays at the Home. We regularly called other kids "queer," but that was simply to denote that they were odd, or weird. It never meant to suggest a sexual orientation ... as if you could orient sex?

The Children's Home had a reward (carrot) and encouragement (stick) system. The rewards consisted of being permitted a bit more leeway in terms of walking around campus, going into town, more honorarium, and better chores. A number of us boys saw these rewards only on rare occasion.

Things We Never Discussed at the Home

The "encouragement" part of the system might be a sound spanking, an opportunity to work at the dairy or farm on Saturday afternoons, or in the Mill grinding feed.

Though we would on occasion get a sound whooping with a strap, paddle, or switch, beatings as such were never occasioned upon us or any of the kids we knew. We were never hit with a fist, kicked, or thrown to the ground by any of the staff or under the direction of the staff by others. Some children may have come to the Home from places where such treatment took place, but it was not accepted or condoned at the Children's Home. Teaching discipline and cooperation was more of a psychological than a physical process, though a strap, switch, and paddle were in full view should there be doubt. The carrot-and-stick approach worked well.

Some would suggest that we lived a sheltered life at the Home. Certainly, that is one way to look at it, but we were busy learning what is good about life. Looking back, we spent our time working, learning, and playing sports. We didn't have time to wallow in self-pity or to try to make ourselves look better than someone else at his or her expense because we lacked confidence in ourselves. We were busy growing and achieving. The only free time we had was spent on adventures as related throughout this book. We practiced our ability to become invisible, to become one with the darkness. Of course, the Home Mothers had already mastered those abilities in addition to being able to see us in any of our sneak-about disguises.

We were quick to discuss any pending punishment and to whom it was directed and for what. That kind of news traveled fast. Pending punishment rumors had a way of dispersing crowds or causing us to change plans for an upcoming adventure. Unfortunately, we were pulled into the punishment grid by virtue of association. It usually meant cleaning out barns or working in the ditch on a Saturday.

We discussed the war, especially the Korean War. We were told of its horror, but also of its necessity. One of our older brothers served there. We wrote letters back and forth. We shared his letters with the others at the Home.

Those were simpler times. A time when honesty, integrity, and earned rewards prevailed. It was a time of sacrifice and a time of triumph. It was America at her finest.

A Children's Home Alumna's Challenge to Our Society

The history of children's homes and orphanages is a rich legacy to thousands of children who grew up there, and many thousands more who have parents, grandparents, and great-grandparents who became the patriarchs and matriarchs of their families. Though imperfect, these havens for children were born from an extraordinary concern, turned to passion, for homeless and helpless children.

Without a professional study or staff, or what would be considered today as qualified designers or administers, churches and social organizations labored to provide communities based on the safety, security and well-being of children. Campuses were established that induced an environment of family and a sense of belonging, nourishing mind, body, and soul. These campuses were financed and maintained by churches, wealthy benefactors, businesses, and thousands of $5.00 a month contributions from farmers, teachers, Sunday school classes, welders, and many more who simply wanted to help in a small way to support children.

Today's government-funded programs would do well to study the children's homes and orphanages of the 1900s. The intent of children's homes and orphanages extended far beyond keeping children safe. These homes for children were not filled with rag-tag, sad street urchins who grew into homeless untrained and uneducated adults. From the day a child entered a children's home, all the activities of his/her life were centered on helping them become a whole, happy and functioning adult.

Education, life skills, work ethic, social behavior, loyalty, faithfulness, respect, play, community involvement and self-worth were all instilled in each child. Sound like a utopia? It wasn't. But what childhood, no matter how close to perfect, is?

Most children would have preferred that circumstances had been different, that they could have had a normal start to their young lives. However, whatever brought them to "the home" no longer defined them as individuals and certainly not as a limit on their future. The trauma that brought them there was not perpetuated by the trauma of not having the security and stability of "a home" – a place to belong.

What children's homes and orphanages were was a safety net that gave children the means to be the best they could be. They gave children a history, a family, and a support system that extended into their adult life, even into their senior years.

Today, life is different for children needing out-of-home care. Most children growing up in children's homes and orphanages were not truly orphaned, just as today's children. However, now these children are involved in a social service child welfare program operated by the state and federal government. Professionals decide their fate, and it has been the professional opinion that children's homes and orphanages are an inferior and unacceptable placement for a child. Professionals tell us that the best placement is family foster care, which may involve many years, and many different foster families, kin-ship care, or treatment centers before a child is adopted or "age out" of the system at age 18. Professionals tell us that to separate siblings for placement is an acceptable way of providing a family-oriented form of out-of-home care. Professionals have levied unfair and unneeded restrictions, regulations and requirements on what they term "institutions" along with unfounded criticism of campus based placement of children. Most institutions such as children's homes and orphanages have become temporary housing for children that have developed so many problems and labels that they can no longer function in a "normal" family environment.

Society has bought all this social change advocated by professionals and government ... hook, line, and sinker.

There is a low rumble of questioning as to the outcomes of the current system. That rumbling has grown into a small number of private citizens who are finding innovative ways of providing and financing out-of-home care for a small number of children. Many of these alternatives involve creating a small community (a campus) that considers the future of children and the things they need to become a functioning adult. Embracing the child while feeding his potential.

As a society, we need to become aware of what happens to children who experience the trauma of needing a family, a home, a place to belong. If it is our hope for these children to have a chance at a better childhood and a better life, then we should consider them as we would our own. What would we want for our children? Would we depend solely on a government program? Would we pay our taxes and consider the job done? Would we want our children to be raised by policy?

Speaking for thousands, I would want for my child that which I had. A history, a shared memory, the skills and the hope I was blessed with. A place I still feel a sense of belonging.

Deborah Edge,
Daughter, sister, wife, mother, grandparent, great-grand-
    parent, aunt, and friend
Entrepreneur, child advocate, founder of two endowed chil-
    dren's foundations
Grateful alumna of the Methodist Children's Home of
    Winston-Salem, NC

Some Observations

S ome observations extending beyond two decades reveal some changed trends in what is generally termed institutional care of children. These changed trends have to do both with the supporting constituency and the supported children.

It is gratifying to note that the trend of thinking on the part of supporting friends now encourages the idea that some of the best is not too good for the parentless child. Instead of castoffs, misfitted, and unused materials, provision is now made more than ever before for securing substantial and well-suited equipment and supplies. The thinking is becoming more manifest that the parentless child, already deprived of some conditions that a normal child ought to be privileged to enjoy, should not be further penalized by too much deprivations and inferior accommodations.

Child caring institutions, now more generally called "Homes" rather than "Orphanages," are being constructed with fewer children to the building and attended by more talented leadership. Better financial support has enabled child caring administrators to make larger investments in more resourceful directors. It has been our observation that the greatest penalty inflicted upon the institutional child has been connected with poor leadership. Too often the child, directed by different people at different times, suffers because of antagonistic and uncooperative directors. This is being remedied.

Children in most child caring institutions nowadays are exposed to the surrounding social influences more than formerly. In most instances the children in homes for children go to school off the campus. In some instances they go to Sunday School and church away from the home campus. Opportunities for social and recreational enjoyment are more frequently provided away from the campus. Some of these outside contacts bring inside problems. The "institutional child," often referred to as a "shut-in," now has many opportunities for picking up much of the "new freedom" that prevails with children from poorly directed private homes, and thereby secures an assertiveness that too often tends towards going in the wrong direction. Resourceful leadership is needed to cope with such a situation.

As the trend for better treatment and better direction of the institutional child has accumulated, attended as it has been with increased financial support, other causes, particularly with church institutions, have called attention to comparative expenditures, tending to establish a connection that too much money is being spent on the parentless child. Too often this contention is presented by church leaders who are charged with the responsibility of raising funds for less popular but deserving causes.

The Children's Home management has striven to assume a "middle of the road" position in regard to the rearing of its children. We think we have not been extravagant with our friends' money. We have not gone to extreme positions in trying to meet what is sometimes termed ideal standardization. We have not reduced the number of children per building as much as is recommended by such agencies. Instead we have invested more money in better leaders. The type of our leadership has been greatly improved in the run of two decades. A better output of children is our constant challenge.

Taken from The Home Chronicle, September 1951, Vol. XXIII No. 9
O. V. (Pop) Woosley, Superintendent 1930-1954

Children's Homes
Represent Opportunity

Matthew 25:40
And the King shall answer and say unto them,
Verily I say unto you, Inasmuch as ye have done it unto one
of the least of these my brethren, ye have done it unto me.

There have been discussions about the value of "orphanages" like the Children's Home. Can they work in today's society, will they work in our current system of health care and public assistance? Is there a proven method for success? To these questions, I can give a resounding "Yes." It is not only possible, but it may be a crucial element in caring for and teaching our lost generation of children.

Certainly, many aspects must be considered when trying to make this happen. Human services organizations nationwide could take a page from the *Chronicles of the Children's Home*. In fact, they should take all of the pages. The *Chronicles* are a wonderful presentation of a proven method of the proper care and raising of children. These could apply to any family, regardless of size or circumstance. They should be in every library in the country and should be required study for people seeking degrees in human services.

The *Chronicles* are a blueprint, a map, of not only the structure of the organization, but of its day-to-day workings ... and enormous success.

Blackberry Rain

In a time when we are plagued with a political system ripe with corruption, a society whose very fabric is challenged by laziness and incompetence, and where future generations are deprived of care, education, and a loving environment, these *Chronicles* are a miracle of great proportion.

We have been given an opportunity to save a generation of children based upon a proven blueprint. This didn't evolve over a few short years and wasn't honed to perfection by people seeking recognition or treasure. This is the culmination of many years of hard, dedicated work, and the patience of saints.

There are thousands of us standing as a living testament to the purity, simplicity, and genius of this action. It was conceived out of caring and dedicated to the betterment of children in difficult circumstances. This is not charity; this is not a handout. This is a seed that represents the future, and when properly nourished and encouraged, it will thrive and make all around who see and touch it prosper. It is a hand offered to a small, scared child; it is a smile filled with energy that burns bright and strong. It is the hand of God.

There are those who have never seen the wonder of a Children's Home graduating class. Once you have been there, once you have been touched by their inner strength and outer compassion, and their quiet determination, you will know that there is a place for Children's Homes in today's society.

We have over 500 brothers and sisters and stay in contact with many of them regularly through personal visits, over the phone, via letters and email, and at annual reunions. Many of the children who grew up at the Home met their life's partners there. Our brother Sam met his soul mate, Charlena Tanner, there and they were married after they left the Home. The Home children have led happy, productive lives and have raised wonderful, caring families. All of us are proud to say that we grew up at the Children's Home in Winston-Salem, North Carolina. In fact, I do so every time I get a chance. Others from the many Homes across this nation express the same joy and pride about their Home. Neither we nor they espouse religious dogma or insist that our Home was better than another's. We share the silent bond that holds us together: "The greatest good to the greatest number."

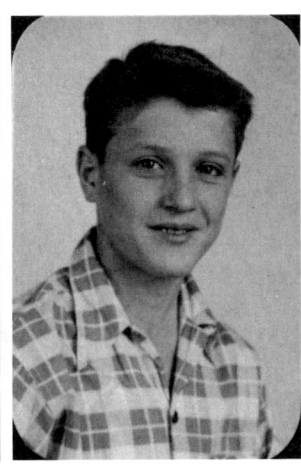

Fred and Charlena Tanner (left) and Sam Murdock (right). Sam and Charlena married after they left the Home, and are an example of the continuing and lifelong relationships that formed at the Home.

So, when you hear someone who doesn't think Children's Homes are the answer, put them in touch with people who were fortunate enough to have grown up in one. You'll be amazed at how proud, and how happy we are … true Americans who have contributed and continue to contribute to this great country! We are hard working, fiercely independent, stand for what is right, will not tolerate or excuse incompetent leaders, and will stand shoulder to shoulder with the weak and infirm. We are the product of American generosity. We bear the torch of hope for the future … and we proudly pass it along.

Homecoming, 2009.